A GUIDE TO
The Whole Writing Process

A GUIDE TO

The Whole Writing Process

Second Edition

JACK BLUM
Freshman Writing Program
University of Southern California

CAROLYN BRINKMAN
Long Beach City College

ELIZABETH HOFFMAN
Freshman Writing Program
University of Southern California

DAVID PECK
California State University, Long Beach

HOUGHTON MIFFLIN COMPANY   Boston
Dallas   Geneva, Illinois   Palo Alto   Princeton, New Jersey

For Eric, Joe, Sarah, and Shelagh

Acknowledgments begin on page 261.

Cover image produced by Slide Graphics of New England, Inc. Copyright 1987.

Printed in the U.S.A.

Library of Congress Catalog Card Number: 87-81366

Student's Edition ISBN: 0-395-38011-1

Instructor's Annotated Edition ISBN: 0-395-45037-3

GHIJ—RM—954

Contents

PART II/RESOURCES

Preface

A Guide to the Whole Writing Process, Second Edition, provides a concrete and encouraging approach for beginning writers. In a field dominated by texts that deal primarily with grammar and mechanics, *A Guide* stands out because it is structured to introduce students to the *process* of writing. *A Guide* presents the process as recursive and individual to each writer and situation, and engages students in the fundamental processes of invention and prewriting, focusing, global organization, drafting, and revision. Throughout the book, exercises and activities reinforce the writing strategies presented in *A Guide.* Several features further distinguish *A Guide* from other texts:

Process approach. Unlike textbooks that move students slowly from sentence drills through paragraph exercises to actually writing papers, *A Guide* begins by having students produce whole pieces of writing. Grammar, syntax, mechanics, and paragraph structure are treated throughout in the context of their effect upon the whole paper, rather than isolating them from the writing process.

Writer's Notebook. Chapter 2, "The Writer's Notebook," allows students to begin writing in a nonthreatening context and to start collecting a useful body of their own writing. The notebook encourages critical thinking and reading-based writing early in the course.

Invention and prewriting. Prewriting is shown as a tentative and exploratory first step in meaningful writing, not as a neat and rigid outline of something fully thought out. This approach helps students break free from the notion that writing is something they must get right the first time. To help get students started, *A Guide* presents three different methods of prewriting: *brainstorming, clustering,* and *discovery writing.*

Experiential vs. analytical writing. Rather than divorcing experiential writing from analytical writing, *A Guide* demonstrates their interdependence. Although students begin by writing about their personal experience in Chapter 2, this is the first step towards *decentering,* a concept developed fully in Chapter 7. Decentering requires students to analyze their experience and draw on public sources of information to support their personal views. Students learn that writing offers a powerful means of understanding their own lives and the world around them, as well as a way to communicate their ideas to others.

Revision. Students discover that a revision involves more than a search for surface errors. By using a two-stage process of description and evaluation introduced in Chapter 8, students learn to revise their own writing effectively. *Example essays* further illustrate how revision works. Chapter 9 focuses on sentence-level revision, enabling students to develop syntactic fluency in their own writing by learning how to combine and expand sentences. Chapter 10 takes a functional approach to grammatical conventions, treating them as vital to the later stages of the writing process.

FEATURES OF THE SECOND EDITION

Although the second edition of *A Guide to the Whole Writing Process* retains the philosophy and intent of the first edition, it incorporates many changes that reflect users' and reviewers' suggestions.

☐ *New overview chapter.* Chapter 1, "Looking Ahead," gives instructors and students a clear overview of the writing process and describes the structure of the book.

☐ *Improved organization and design.* Early chapters have been reorganized, and all chapters now open with an outline of the important concepts to be covered. Many of the exercises, group activities, and writing activities are completely redesigned, making them easier for instructors to assign. Diagrams now clarify material in Chapter 5 (organizational patterns), Chapter 6 (levels of support), and Chapters 9 and 10 (sentence grammar and usage, and word order).

☐ *More attention to reading-based writing.* The section on summarizing and responding to readings in Chapter 2 prepares students for the process of decentering, discussed in depth in Chapter 7. Chapter 8 further reinforces this process with new material that helps students read and respond to classmates' papers.

☐ *More attention to focusing and arranging material.* Chapter 4 now demonstrates concretely the process of finding focus and order in students' prewriting. To help students visualize and understand the structure of whole writing, Chapter 5 uses schematic diagrams to illustrate a variety of organizational patterns.

☐ *More comprehensive treatment of revision.* Chapter 8, "Revising the Whole Paper," helps students develop introductions and conclusions and use transitions. Chapters 9 and 10 discuss sentence-level revision in more detail.

☐ *Expanded chapters on grammar and syntax.* Chapters 9 and 10 now include more on complete versus incomplete sentences, verb problems, and exercises for punctuation skills.

ACKNOWLEDGMENTS

In its second edition as in its first, *A Guide* represents a collective effort. Whatever improvements it displays are in large part the result of the many comments offered by students and instructors, particularly Allen Bundy, Larry Gouldrup, Wendy Greenstein, Fred Masback, and Charles Pomeroy. We would also like to express our appreciation to those whose reviews of the first edition have guided our revision:

Sandra Clark, Anderson College

Mike Cooper, Westark Community College

David D. Dahnke, North Harris County College, South Campus

Francine DeFrance, Cerritos College

Suellyn Duffey, Ohio State University

Jake Gaskins, Southeast Missouri State University

Ann M. Green, Jackson Community College

Walt Klarner, Johnson County Community College

Keith Miller, Arizona State University

Kathy Osterholm, Clarion University of Pennsylvania

Geoffrey Platt, Hunter College—CUNY

Sandra Roy

Mary Kay Tirrell, California State University, Fullerton

Steven Waterworth, El Camino College

Gloria Weintraub, Fullerton College

Joan Wilson, City College of San Francisco

J.B., C.B., E.H., D.P.

*A Letter to Students*___

We have written *A Guide to the Whole Writing Process* to help you gain skill and confidence in your writing. We hope that our approach helps you to see that writing is not some unsolvable mystery but, instead, a process you *can* learn as you write your way through this book.

Students often need to discover the worth of their own writing and to become aware of how writing skills are acquired. We help you develop the writing skills necessary for both school and work by showing you how to explore your ideas and express yourself and by involving you in the writing process from the very first pages of this book.

A Guide encourages you to develop an individual writing process and learn how to respond to the demands of various writing situations. It allows you to experience the recursive, "back-and-forth" nature of the writing process so that you can understand why good papers are not produced in a one-shot burst of energy at 7 A.M., but in a process of rethinking and rewriting a topic through several stages and drafts.

In *A Guide* you will begin with *whole pieces* of writing, rather than just sentences and short paragraphs. You start by recording your own ideas and experiences in a Writer's Notebook and then go on to practice techniques of invention, arrangement, and revision that will enable you to develop your ideas more fully and express them more clearly.

Chapters 1–7 of *A Guide* present activities that engage you in writing, from your first ideas to your final draft. Chapter 1, "Looking Ahead," serves as a frame for the entire textbook by introducing you to the ideas that underlie the text's approach to writing and by providing you with a brief outline of every chapter. Chapter 2, "The Writer's Notebook," gets you writing immediately within the familiar context of your Writer's Notebook. In Chapter 3, "Exploring Topics," you learn three prewriting techniques to help you develop ideas for your writing. Chapter 4, "From Exploratory Writing to Paper," shows you how to focus and organize the ideas you have developed, and Chapter 5, "Shaping and Arranging Ideas," introduces a number of patterns you may use to structure your writing. Chapter 6, "Strengthening Your Support," helps you develop the habit of supporting your ideas with relevant evidence and detailed language. In Chapter 7,

"Inquiring Further," you learn how to probe more deeply into topics by decentering. In this process, you learn to move beyond your own initial perspective on a topic by considering views offered by outside sources of information.

Chapters 8–10 of *A Guide* stress various kinds of revision, and you may turn to each of these chapters as you begin revising complete drafts of your papers. Chapter 8, "Revising the Whole Paper," shows you how to read your own writing analytically and make any necessary large-scale changes so that you can more effectively address your readers. Chapter 9, "Revising Sentences," focuses on combining, expanding, or tightening sentences. Chapter 10, "Identifying and Correcting Errors," shows you how to revise for conventional mechanics, usage, and punctuation.

We hope that *A Guide* will help you not only to write with greater confidence and ease but also to discover the value and power that writing can have in your life.

J.B., C.B., E.H., D.P.

A GUIDE TO
The Whole
Writing
Process

Part I
The Writing Process

Chapter 1
Looking Ahead

- Thinking About the Writing Process
- Chapter-by-Chapter Overview of the Textbook

THINKING ABOUT THE WRITING PROCESS

Many people fear writing and see it as mysterious and impossibly difficult. This book was written to help students overcome such feelings and see that writing is a process that can be learned. Before you start to work your way through this book, you may find it worthwhile to consider the following ideas, which are fundamental to the book. If you know more about the writing process and about what writing can do in your life, you may feel much more encouraged to write.

1. **Writing is a way of thinking.**

   Getting things down in writing helps you examine experiences, sort through information, and analyze ideas in order to understand and make better sense of the world. For example, if you must discuss a problem with a boss or instructor, you will be much better prepared if you write down beforehand the issues and points you wish to make.

2. **Writing is an act of communication.**

   Writing takes on greater importance when you begin to see it as a way to make yourself heard, to persuade people to see something your way, to argue for ideas you believe in, to change things. This book is based on the principle that you and other student writers have something important to say and that writing is a powerful way to communicate your ideas and experiences to others.

3. **You have a natural sense of language and of what language can do.**

   Most people think they know nothing about grammar, and yet they *use* grammar every time they speak, listen, read, or write. For example, you would never say, "The cat from jumped the table," even though you may not be able to explain *why* it is grammatically incorrect. As a speaker of the English language (even if you are not a native speaker), you probably know more than you realize about how the language operates. You can use this knowledge to improve your writing.

4. You can learn to write with greater confidence and ease.

Many students are anxious about writing because they feel that they have nothing to say or that they don't know how to get their ideas down on paper. In fact, because you have experienced, observed, thought—in short, lived—you can draw on a wealth of material for your writing. By writing frequently and by learning more about the writing process, you will become a more confident writer.

5. Writing is not a neat, orderly, step-by-step process.

Writing is the messy process of finding focus and order in a profusion and chaos of ideas. This process is necessarily interior, taking place largely in the writer's head. For this reason, it is difficult to break the whole activity into simple, well-defined steps that would work for all writers.

6. By studying different writing strategies, you can develop a writing process that works for you.

This textbook models a variety of techniques for exploring, focusing, and ordering your ideas and for revising your writing. By experimenting with different techniques, you can determine which ones work best for you. Remember, the writing process is different for different people and different tasks.

7. Revision is an ongoing process that begins when you first start thinking about a writing topic.

Many people think revision is just proofreading—identifying and correcting errors in a paper that is nearly complete. In fact, revision is the process of reseeing your writing, and it begins as soon as you start thinking about your topic. Any time you consider changing an idea, a plan of organization, a sentence or word, you are revising.

8. Although correctness is important, errors are a natural part of the writing process and of learning to write.

Every writer makes mistakes, but the experienced writer learns not to worry about them until the later stages of the writing process. Worrying about errors too soon can interfere with the more important matters of developing ideas and organizing your writing.

9. You should remain at the center of whatever you write.

Some writing, such as the academic writing you are asked to do in college, may require you to write about topics that seem quite far removed from your immediate experience, but all good writing reflects an individual writer's encounter with the ideas central to a topic. It is therefore important to develop your own perspective on topics and to keep your own voice and convictions at the center of your writing.

CHAPTER-BY-CHAPTER OVERVIEW OF THE TEXTBOOK ⸻⸻⸻

The purpose of this book is to help you develop your own writing process. To do this, it is useful for you to look at the different parts of that process, each of which is presented in a separate chapter of this book. The following chapter-by-chapter outline will provide you with an overview of the whole writing process.

Chapter 2: The Writer's Notebook

This chapter will show you how to set up a Writer's Notebook, in which, throughout the semester, you can develop your ideas, record and respond to the ideas of others, and practice writing.

Chapter 3: Exploring Topics

In this chapter, you will learn three techniques—brainstorming, clustering, and discovery writing—that will help you explore topics when you are writing papers and reports.

Chapter 4: From Exploratory Writing to Paper: Focusing and Ordering Your Material

This chapter explains how to move from exploration writing to a finished paper by limiting the topic, deciding what point to make about that topic, and preparing a rough plan of the paper.

Chapter 5: Shaping and Arranging Ideas

In this chapter, you will look more closely at organization by exploring different patterns for arranging the ideas that go into your paper. Included is a section on how to expand a rough plan into an outline.

Chapter 6: Strengthening Your Support

In order to convince your reader of your main point, you must have strong support for that point. This chapter will show you ways to strengthen your support through the use of detailed evidence and vivid language.

Chapter 7: Inquiring Further

To produce effective writing, you often need to go beyond your initial impressions about a topic. This chapter describes ways to analyze a topic more carefully and to use information from outside sources.

Chapter 8: Revising the Whole Paper

This chapter will show you how to read a piece of writing critically so that you can evaluate what needs to be changed in order to clarify its meaning. You will also learn revision techniques that will help you in rewriting.

Chapter 9: Revising Sentences

This chapter focuses on sentence-level revision. You will learn ways to combine, expand, and tighten sentences to stengthen and clarify them.

Chapter 10: Identifying and Correcting Errors

The final chapter offers ways to identify and correct errors in mechanics, usage, punctuation, and sentence structure.

Writing Activity 1   *Examining Your Attitudes Toward Writing*

Think about your own history as a writer. In a short piece of writing, respond to the following questions:

1. In general, how do you feel about writing?
2. What are your strengths as a writer?
3. What are some of the changes you would like to make in your writing process?

Now read through the list of ideas on the first page of this chapter and respond to these questions:

4. Which of the ideas do you strongly agree with? Why?
5. Which of the ideas do you disagree with or find puzzling? Why?

Finally, read through the chapter-by-chapter overview on pp. 3–4 and respond to this question:

6. Which chapters may be particularly helpful to you?

Your instructor may ask you to discuss your responses with other class members.

Chapter 2
The Writer's Notebook _____

THE WRITER'S NOTEBOOK _____

What Is a Writer's Notebook?

A Writer's Notebook is a place to explore your own ideas, to record and respond to the ideas of others, and to practice writing. By writing every day or every other day in your notebook, you will become more confident as a writer and will improve your writing and your critical thinking skills. By the end of the course, you will have a substantial collection of writing. In addition, some entries from your notebook may be expanded into papers for class assignments.

How Do I Keep a Writer's Notebook?

You keep a Writer's Notebook by making regular entries, both in and outside of class. Chapter 2 is a resource chapter that you can return to throughout the course whenever you need ideas for notebook entries. Date every entry. A loose-leaf notebook works well because you can discard or rearrange pages and can easily remove any entry you wish to share or turn in to your instructor. To organize your Writer's Notebook efficiently, use dividers to separate sections containing different kinds of entries.

WRITER'S NOTEBOOK ENTRIES

Writing from Topic Lists

One type of entry is a response to a topic suggested by your instructor or chosen from the five lists of potential topics included below. You may wish to modify one of the topics or use it as a springboard to a topic of your own.

This is a brief entry one writer wrote on a topic from the first list:

A Significant Memory   *May1*

Every time I smell fresh cut grass on a warm day I start thinking about when I ran cross country back in high school. Every time we were running—usually August through the end of October—it would be warm and the janitors would be mowing the lawn. So today when I am walking through a grass area which has been mowed recently, automatically my memories flash back to the times when my friends and I were running along. We would always start out bunched in a pack, but we gradually sorted ourselves out into small groups and some solitary runners. Sometimes I liked to run with someone else. We didn't talk, but through some unspoken agreement, we would begin to run in unison, taking the same length strides. Most of the time, though, I preferred to run off by myself. My body seemed to be under its own control. I paid just enough attention to make sure I didn't trip in a gopher hole. My mind was free to wander far from the field I was running across.

Writing Activity 1   Pick a topic from one of the following lists and make it the subject of an entry in your Writer's Notebook. Write freely and don't worry about making mistakes. Read over the entry after you finish writing and mark any passages you especially like.

Topic List No. 1: Memories

1. A memorable present
2. A family tradition
3. Grandmothers
4. A car I have owned
5. Ways to escape
6. Something I have collected
7. A significant memory
8. Family stories I've heard over and over again
9. A strange or eerie experience
10. An unusual place I have lived
11. Stories I've been told about a historical event that occurred before I was born
12. A time in my childhood I would like to live through again

Topic List No. 2: Impressions and Observations

1. Inside a church or hospital
2. A street corner
3. Laundromats
4. Derelicts/street people
5. Taking the bus or subway
6. Commercials that irritate me
7. A valued possession
8. My strongest quality
9. Getting older
10. Something that helps when I'm feeling sick or depressed
11. A place where I like to spend time
12. Something that makes me stand out from other people in a unique way

Topic List No. 3: Relationships

1. A difficult boss
2. Someone I miss
3. An important relationship I have with someone from a younger or older generation
4. A person I know who has aged gracefully
5. A person who has had a significant impact on my life

6. Changes I would like to make in the way my family does things
7. A group I have belonged to that had a significant effect on me
8. An opinion I hold that my relatives would disagree with
9. Different roles I play in my life (student, employee, friend, brother or sister, neighbor and so on)

Topic List No. 4: Problems and Challenges

1. Taking exams
2. Something that irritates me or wastes my time
3. Something I fear
4. Being broke
5. A time when I felt like an outsider
6. Something I was discouraged from doing
7. The worst job I have ever had
8. A time I encountered prejudice
9. A difficult time that I survived
10. A dilemma in my life that I have never completely resolved
11. A concept in one of my classes that I have difficulty understanding
12. An important goal and my plans for achieving it

Topic List No. 5: Acquiring Experience and Knowledge

1. Learning to drive a car
2. Lessons I have taken
3. An experience that taught me something important
4. Something I have learned to do very well
5. Information I need to gather in order to make a wise choice about something I wish to buy or do
6. An experience I have had that others could learn from
7. A teacher, coach, or boss who motivated me to learn
8. A movie, book, or television program that gave me new insight into some issue
9. An accomplishment or award I worked hard to achieve
10. Principles or standards that guide the way I conduct my life

Topic List No. 6: Turning Points and Significant Moments

1. An important phone call
2. A moment of danger
3. A moment of friendship

4. A holiday that is significant in my life

5. A ceremony or formal act that marked a change in my life

6. A difficult decision

7. Something I have done or seen someone else do that required courage

8. Something I have done that made a difference to someone else

9. An idea I encountered in a college course that changed the way I think

10. Something I have done that could be considered unusual for someone my age

11. A controversial issue I have changed my mind about

12. A time when my life changed direction

Topic List No. 7:   Examining Events and Issues

1. Something that is done differently now from the way it was done when I was younger

2. A recent news story that caught my attention

3. An event of national or international importance that I will never forget

4. Things most commonly worried about by the people in my age group

5. How my life will be different from my parents' lives

6. How my childhood was different from the childhoods of today's children

7. Stereotypes that cause difficulties

8. A movie, book, television program, or concert that I believe has a negative effect on the audience

9. An idea I have encountered in one of my classes with which I strongly agree or disagree

10. Changes in the local economy and the effect of those changes on the community

11. An invention or technological advance that made a difference in my life

12. Something in our society I consider to be an injustice and my thoughts on what could be done to change it

Generating Your Own Topic List

Writers usually feel the most commitment to topics that reflect their own particular interests and knowledge; therefore a list of your own topics is a useful entry in your Writer's Notebook. Throughout the course, keep an ongoing record of topics you would like to explore. These can come from personal experience, from work in other classes, and from reading or observations. Refer to this list when you need a topic for a regular notebook entry. The list you generate may also suggest topics for papers for this or another class.

Writing Activity 2   Keep an ongoing list of possible topics for entries on a separate page of your writer's notebook. Add to this list throughout the course. Start by listing every topic that comes to mind as you go through the following categories:

> Significant experiences in my life
>
> Things I am strongly in favor of
>
> Things I am strongly opposed to
>
> Things I would like to know more about
>
> Things I am curious or confused about
>
> Things I would like to change
>
> Ideas that intrigue or interest me

Writing Activity 3   Pick a topic from your own list and make it the subject of an entry in your notebook. Read over the entry after you finish writing and mark any passages you especially like.

Freewriting

In a freewriting entry, you write without stopping. Write on anything you happen to be thinking about for at least ten minutes without worrying about spelling or punctuation or finding the perfect word. Don't stop writing if you run out of ideas on one topic; a freewriting entry does not have to be on just one topic. Use freewriting to warm up whenever you have trouble getting started. Once you get started, you may find yourself reluctant to stop.

Below is an example of a freewriting entry:

> Writing in the classroom is easy. But here at home, there are too many distractions. I'm thinking about getting up and grabbing a Coke. A door just slammed. I wonder if there's something good to watch on television. It's easy to just blank out in front of the tv and not have to think. But I did watch something last night that got me thinking — a show called "Fight Back" that tells people how to

take action when they feel that they have been cheated by some store or company. I know people have rights and should be able to get something done when they buy something that is dangerous or doesn't work. But it seems as if people now are just looking for any little mistake so they can jump on the person they think is responsible, and this attitude just makes life harder for everyone. I know this from working as a cashier at McDonald's. Things get really hectic there. But sometimes a customer makes a big scene over being shortchanged one penny. This is carrying consumer rights <u>too far</u>.

Writing Activity 4 Write freely in your Writer's Notebook for ten to twenty minutes on any idea that is moving through your mind. If you have trouble getting started, try responding to the question, "What's on my mind today?" If the only thing on your mind is doing this exercise, write about that.

When you stop writing, read over what you have written.

1. Underline any part of your entry that you especially like.
2. Star (*) any part of your entry you could write more about.

Expanding an Entry

Another type of Writer's Notebook entry is an expansion of a previous entry. Some entries may have little in them worth pursuing, but others are worth spending more time on. Sometimes an entry can be expanded and developed into an interesting and informative paper.

The following techniques will help you identify parts of an entry that could be expanded:

1. Read through an entry and mark any section that stands out and catches your attention.
2. Mark any section that you know more about and to which you could add details.
3. Ask someone else to read your entry and identify the strongest or most interesting part.

On the next page is a Writer's Notebook entry one student wrote on the topic "Something That Irritates Me."

I'm irritated about the hassle registration has been. Waiting in line to get classes is the worst. If you don't have all the paperwork just right you can forget about getting the classes. They also catch people who have not paid their bills when they go to get an i.d. The people working at registration treat you like a criminal. They act like they are doing you a big favor to let you register. <u>*It's a real trick to learn how to survive*</u>✳ <u>*around this place.*</u> *It's a terrible way to start the semester. I've stood in line for hours and gone back twice and I still don't have everything straightened out.*

After reading over the above entry, the student marked one part of the entry he found interesting. In the next entry, the writer expands the idea that "it's a real trick to learn how to survive around this place" by showing specific techniques for handling the college bureaucracy.

Surviving the College Bureaucracy

Registration is a hassle. But learning a few tricks about how to handle the bureaucracy can help you survive here. First, learn to plan ahead. Everything is easier when you don't try to do something on the last possible day. When you are registering or adding classes, have all the forms filled out right. Having all the correct signatures will get you through the red-tape. Even if you don't think you need the signatures, get them anyway. It doesn't hurt to have more signatures than you really need. It's easier in the long run. Check that you have paid all your debts to the university. If you haven't, you won't get an I.D. and later they won't issue you a diploma. Save all your receipts from every transaction in case you need to prove you have taken care of something. Carry your student I.D. at all times. Almost everything you do at this college requires your student I.D. Since much of your time in college is spent waiting in long lines, you should become an expert at standing in lines. Bring a book to read or some homework to do. Last week I read the whole first chapter in my history book while waiting in line. Talk to the other people standing in line with you. You might learn some useful information or even meet someone really interesting. Finally, don't expect to get any cooperation at this school if you continually get angry at the people who work here. They feel hassled too and the best way to make things go easier for you is to take everything in stride and keep a smile on your face.

Writing Activity 5   Read through several Writer's Notebook entries and select one you would like to write more about. Mark a section of the entry that particularly stands out and use that section to begin a new entry.

Writing from Reading:
Commonplace Entries

Commonplace entries are short quotations that you collect and copy into your Writer's Notebook. The quotations come from books, magazines, or newspapers and contain material with interesting facts, intriguing ideas, or a striking style. Compiling a collection of commonplace entries helps you appreciate the way other writers use language and helps you practice the conventions of spelling and punctuation. In addition, a commonplace entry may suggest an idea for a paper.

Proofread each commonplace entry to insure that you have copied it correctly. An efficient way to proofread is to have someone else read the original passage aloud (indicating capitals and punctuation) while you check your copy. Another method is to exchange copies with someone else in the class and take turns reading the original aloud while you check the accuracy of the other person's copy.

Add a response to each commonplace entry giving your reaction to the issues raised in the quotation.

Below is a collection of commonplace entries.

We have to face it: boredom is here, lodged in the culture, and it's spreading by the minute. It is the most splendid of ironies, really. For America is richer in options and entertainments than any society at any point in recorded history. We have access to every resource and vice. But go out and check for yourself. Walk through your city or town for just one day with your eyes open. . . . Wherever you turn, fingers are drumming, gazes are detached, and eyes are wandering.

> Sven Birkerts, Boston Phoenix
> July 22, 1986

Response: After reading this, I have taken more notice of how bored many of the people around me seem to be. I know I sometimes sit around doing nothing or watching t.v. because I don't feel like making an effort to do something more interesting.

If a man does not keep pace with his companions, perhaps it is because he hears a different drummer. Let him step to the music which he hears, however measured or far away.

> Henry David Thoreau, Walden,
> Norton Critical Editions, 1966, p.215.

Response: I've heard this before but I never knew where it came from. I like the idea that it's o.k. for someone to be different. I also like the way the lines flow when I read them aloud.

The fat content of fast-food hamburgers commonly ranges from the equivalent of slightly more than three teaspoons (13 grams) to more than 11 teaspoons (45 grams).

> Ross Laboratories Dietetic Currents
> Newsletter, 1986

Response: It's disturbing to read that there is this much fat in a hamburger, especially since I eat at a lot of fast-food restaurants.

Writing Activity 6 On a separate piece of paper in your Writer's Notebook, carefully copy the following passage, including the source. Then proofread your copy, using one of the methods described above. Make any necessary corrections. Add a response giving your reaction to the passage.

Space Pets |

If R2–D2 seemed cute enough to have around the house, says psychologist Philip R. Harris, that's significant. In the future, a lot of lonely people in space will become emotionally attached to their robots. In the early stages of space colonization, "it's not going to be feasible to send up dogs and cats," Harris says. The cost of getting them—and their life-support systems—up into orbit and beyond will be too high. But this won't matter, because the robots working on board can double as pets. It's bound to happen. "When you're up in space and pretty much removed and lonely, and you've got these robots that can walk and talk and maybe even look humanlike, why not develop a relationship?" Space engineers can actively encourage these attachments by designing humanlike features and capabilities into the robots.

> *Omni*, October 1985, p. 42.

Writing Activity 7 On a separate piece of paper in your Writer's Notebook, carefully copy the following passage, including the source. Then proofread your copy, using one of the methods described above. Make any necessary corrections. Add a response giving your reaction to the passage.

Excerpt from *Letter from Birmingham Jail* |

How does one determine whether a law is just or unjust? A just law is a man-made code that squares with the moral law or the law of God. An unjust law is a code that is out of harmony with the moral law. To put it in the terms of St. Thomas Aquinas: An unjust law is a human law that is not rooted in internal law and natural law. Any law that uplifts human personality is just. Any law that degrades human personality is unjust. All segregation statutes are unjust because segregation distorts the soul and damages the personality. It gives the segregator a false sense of superiority and the segregated a false sense of inferiority. Segregation, to use the terminology of the Jewish philosopher Martin Buber, substitutes an "I-it" relationship for an "I-thou" relationship and ends up relegating persons to the status of things. Hence segregation is not only politically, economically and sociologically unsound, it is morally wrong and sinful.

> Martin Luther King, *Letter from Birmingham Jail*
> from *Why We Can't Wait*, p. 85.

Writing Activity 8   Compile a collection of commonplace entries in your Writer's Notebook. Select from magazines, newspapers, or books some quotations that appeal to you because of style or content. Copy each quotation into the Commonplace section. Make sure you have copied the quotation accurately and have included the source. Add a response commenting on why you found a particular quotation worth recording.

Writing from Reading: Summary and Response

One way to improve your writing is to do more reading. Through reading the writing of others, you get ideas for your own writing, see different ways to organize a piece of writing, and improve your vocabulary and spelling. You can also improve your reasoning skills by making Writer's Notebook entries in which you summarize and respond to some of your reading.

Notebook entries in which you summarize and respond to your reading are most beneficial if you do them regularly. You can select readings from newspapers, magazines, books, or pamphlets. Try to find material that genuinely interests you. Your instructor may supply some reading selections, and you can also ask instructors in other courses to recommend selections from magazines or books.

Techniques for Writing a Summary

1. Read the selection twice. Underline key sentences or phrases.
2. On a separate piece of paper, answer these questions:
   a. What is the reading selection about? (What is its topic?)
   b. What points does the author make about the topic?
   c. What is the author's main point?
   d. What facts, details, or reasons are used to convince you of that point?
3. Using your responses to the above questions, write the summary. Begin by stating the main point of the selection. Next write down the key ideas the author uses to develop that point. Remember that a summary should be considerably shorter than the original; however, no important ideas should be left out. Use your own words as much as possible, but do not add any ideas that were not in the original.

Techniques for Writing a Personal Response.   In a personal response you explain what *you* think about the ideas in a reading selection. Consider the following questions:

1. Do you agree or disagree with what the selection says?
2. Explain why you agree or disagree.
3. If the selection describes a problem, what possible solutions can you suggest?
4. Why is this selection of interest to you? Would you recommend it to others? Why or why not?

The following notebook entry is a summary and response based on an article about the effects of television on children. For this entry, the writer read through the article twice, and then, using the techniques outlined above, wrote a half-page summary and a half-page response.

Physical Violence Aside, TV's Psychic Violence Is the Real Cause for Alarm | *Herbert Kohl*

There have been a number of studies that have claimed to establish some statistical link between TV and violence. However, these studies establish at best that many poor, lonely, isolated and despairing individuals spend a lot of time looking at TV screens. The causes of the violence that occasionally explodes out of these people come more from already existing psychological, social or economic oppression than from the theatrical violence portrayed on TV. However, TV causes a more serious and pervasive psychic violence in normal, less despairing youngsters who watch TV attentively and regularly. What results from this psychic abuse is the impoverishment of personality and the trivialization of life.

Young people spend a lot of time and energy trying to understand adult behavior and motivation and just how they fit into that world. Imagine what a young viewer of network TV must make of adult behavior on TV. On one evening he or she might see a comedy about people sharing an apartment, arguing all the time and trying to be funny. This comedy is sure to be interrupted by commercials showing adults taking issues such as toilet paper and mouthwash very seriously. With only a minute's pause, a new program begins and the scene shifts to urban violence, also portraying people arguing and fighting—only this time there are no laughs. The violence is punctuated by several sports figures finger-wrestling and drinking beer or a number of attractive women draped across fancy cars. If the young viewers stay up late enough, they may even catch a bit of late-night news where an invasion is followed by a fashion show and a fire—all treated with the same seriousness or flippancy, depending on the "personality" of the news crew. The segments of the programs follow each other so quickly and smoothly that, to a young mind, a battle in Asia and a fire in Chicago could be taking place next door to each other and most probably exist to them at the same level of reality as the detective story or situation comedy.

Television gives our children no close look at the complexity of people or at the depth of feeling that is involved in argumentation, love, violence and all the other subjects of most programs. If adults really behave as the people do on TV, imagine the world that children think they have to prepare themselves to live in. Products would have to be as important as people, feelings as fleeting as every half-hour show, affection merely a matter of comedy or violence. Nuances and crucial subtleties that exist in real adult relationships are missing from the TV adult because everything has to be wrapped up in a half-hour.

Consequently, shades of feeling, reflection on the quality of life and understanding of the fullness of others may be missing from many of our children. I have noticed sadly how many children seem like TV adults; how life for them is a TV comedy or a mystery interspersed with commercials that have become metaphors for their experience. One youngster, for instance, recently replied to one who had pinched her by saying, "Please don't squeeze the Charmin!"

There is absolutely no doubt that we should be concerned about the physical violence in our society and continue to examine TV's relationship to it, but I believe that attention must be given to the psychic violence that is even more pervasive on TV. We must find ways to change the pacing of TV to allow for the development of serious drama and non-shrieking comedy and to provide time for the consideration of people and events in depth. If we do not, we may end up training another generation of TV adults who know what kind of toilet paper or beer to buy, who know how to argue and humiliate others or how to solve a pseudo crime, but who are thoroughly incapable of discussing, much less dealing with, the major social and economic problems that are tearing our society apart.

Los Angeles Times, May 21, 1982

Summary of Reading Selection: Kohl feels that the most serious problem with television is not that it encourages young people to be physically violent but that it causes "psychic violence." It damages children by giving them a warped view of life that does not prepare them for the real world. Commercials tell children that things are more important than people; comedies on TV suggest that life is just a silly joke and all problems can be solved in half an hour; TV news implies that wars and fashion shows are equally important. This psychic abuse results in "the impoverishment of personality and the trivialization of life," and we must find ways to make television a better influence on young people.

Response to Reading Selection: I agree with the author of this article that television gives children a warped view of life. Things in real life are certainly never as simple and clear-cut as they are on television shows. Most things in real life take a lot of time and effort. You have to really want to achieve something and to be willing to work hard and put in the hours necessary to achieve your goal. Nothing happens in one hour like it does on television. Watching television is a way to escape problems rather than facing up to solving the problems. But watching junky shows on television is what people want to do, as proven by the high ratings that junky shows get.

It follows that children tend to watch the same kind of junky television that their parents watch. The solution to what Kohl calls the "psychic violence" caused by television would seem to be higher quality television shows or making sure children watch less television but neither of these solutions is very practical.

Group Activity 1   The following reading selection is an excerpt from an article on computers in *Newsweek*. Read the selection, and then, working in small groups and using the techniques outlined above on p. 15, write a summary of the selection. After you have completed your group summary, your instructor may ask you to share it with the rest of the class or may ask the entire class to collaborate on a revised summary.

And Man Created the Chip | *Merrill Sheils*

A revolution is under way. Most Americans are already well aware of the gee-whiz gadgetry that is emerging, in rapidly accelerating bursts, from the world's high-technology laboratories. But most of us perceive only dimly how pervasive and profound the changes of the next twenty years will be. We are at the dawn of the era of the smart machine—an "information age" that will change forever the way an entire nation works, plays, travels and even thinks. Just as the industrial revolution dramatically expanded the strength of man's muscles and the reach of his hand, so the smart-machine revolution will magnify the power of his brain. But unlike the industrial revolution, which depended on finite resources such as iron and oil, the new information age will be fired by a seemingly limitless resource—the inexhaustible supply of knowledge itself.

The driving force behind the revolution is the development of two fundamental and interactive technologies—computers and integrated circuits. Today, tiny silicon chips half the size of a fingernail are etched with circuitry powerful enough to book seats on jumbo jets (and keep the planes working smoothly in the air), cut complex swatches of fabric with little wastage, help children learn to spell and play chess well enough to beat all but the grandest masters. The new technology means that bits of computing power can be distributed wherever they might be useful—the way small electric motors have become ubiquitous—or combined in giant mainframe computers to provide enormous problem-solving potential.

The explosion is just beginning. In 1979, the world market for microelectronics topped $11 billion. Over the next five years, chip sales are expected to grow by at least 20 percent annually, and the market for microprocessors, entire "computers on a chip," will expand by 50 per cent each year—even though the chips themselves and the computing power they represent are diving in price. As industry officials are fond of remarking, if the automobile industry had improved its technology at the same rate computer science has, it would now be turning out Rolls-Royces that cost no more than $70 apiece.

The transformation will not be easy, for smart machines bring with them the seeds of widespread economic dislocation and social unrest. Eventually, for example, they will make possible the full automation of many factories, displacing millions of blue-collar workers with a new "steel-collar" class. Even office workers will feel the crunch, as smart machines do more and more of the clerical work. Traditional businesses such as television networks and publishing companies will encounter new competition as programmers and advertisers beam information directly into the consumer's home.

But industry experts think these problems can—and will—be solved. In the optimists' scenario, educational programs will retrain displaced workers and equip them with skills suited to the booming new information business. Meanwhile, laymen will grow more and more comfortable with computers as they invade everyday life. And in the end, the smart-machine revolution will do far more to enrich life than most Americans realize. As the industry likes to picture the future, the new technology offers potential solutions to humanity's most intractable problems—the allocation of energy resources, food enough for all, and the worldwide improvement of health care.

Newsweek, June 30, 1980

Writing Activity 9 Read a selection that you have chosen or that has been given to you by your instructor. Write a summary and a personal response to that selection, using the techniques outlined below.

1. Read the selection twice. Underline key sentences or phrases.
2. On a separate piece of paper, answer these questions:
   a. What is the reading selection about?
   b. What points does the author make?
   c. What is the author's main point?
   d. What facts, details, or reasons are used to convince you of that point?
3. Write the summary on a separate page of your notebook. Begin by stating the main point of the selection. Next write down the key ideas the author uses to develop that point. Use your own words as much as possible.
4. Record the following information at the top of the notebook page:
   Author of the selection
   Title
   Name of newspaper or magazine if applicable
   Date and page number

After you have summarized a reading selection and understand the author's ideas, write a personal response explaining what *you* think about those ideas. Consider the following questions:

1. Do you agree or disagree with what the selection says?
2. Explain why you agree or disagree.

3. If the selection describes a problem, what possible solutions can you suggest?

4. Why is this selection of interest to you? Would you recommend it to others? Why or why not?

Writing Activity 10   From a textbook or other written material used in another course you are taking, select an important passage and summarize it, using the techniques described above. Then write a response to the passage, focusing on why this passage is important in the context of that course.

Analyzing Your Writing: Sharing an Entry

When you write something, you may be so close to it that you cannot accurately judge its strengths and weaknesses. By sharing your work with a supportive reader, you can receive valuable feedback. Exchanging papers with a classmate also gives you a chance to see the writing being done by others in the class.

Writing Activity 11   Read through your Writer's Notebook again. Pick an entry you especially like and make a clean copy of it to share with a classmate. Ask your classmate to read the entry and respond to the following questions:

1. What did you like best about this entry?
2. What else would you like to know about the subject of this entry?

Record your classmate's response at the end of your entry; it may give you an idea for an expanded entry.

Analyzing Your Writing: Writer's Inventories

In your Writer's Notebook you have been writing about your ideas and experiences and responding to the ideas of others. Now think, not about the product of your writing, but about the *process* you go through when you write. An inventory of your writing habits can help you determine what changes you can make to become a more effective writer.

Writing Activity 12   Write an entry in your notebook, answering as many of the following questions as you can.

1. How do you think your writing differs from your speech?
2. Where do you like to write? What's the best time of the day for you to write?

3. Do you need quiet to write, or can you write with music or noise in the background?

4. Do you need privacy to write well?

5. Do you write better when you have ample time or when you are under pressure?

6. Describe your writing tools: any special paper, pens?

7. How long does one writing session usually last for you? Do you take breaks? How often? What do you do during breaks?

8. Are there things you do to avoid writing or to delay starting to write?

9. What do you worry about when you write?

10. When you're writing, what do you do to get ideas?

11. What is the easiest way for you to get started?

12. Do you usually talk with anyone about what you have written? Does it help?

13. What do you remember about learning to write when you were in elementary school?

14. What specific people have helped or hindered you as a writer?

15. As a writer, what do you feel you are best at? What aspect of writing do you feel you need to work on?

Group Activity 2   Writing is a solitary activity, but you and other writers can learn more about the process by sharing thoughts about your writing. Sharing your responses to the above writer's inventory, with the whole class or in a small group, can give you a new perspective on the problems writers face and the techniques they use to solve those problems.

Writing Activity 13   Later in the course, after you have completed several assignments, analyze your writing process by taking the following inventory in order to see if any of your writing habits have changed.

Write an entry in your notebook, answering as many of the following questions as possible.

1. What is the best piece of writing you have ever done? What makes it your best?

2. Have you been surprised by anything you have written?

3. Have you learned more about a subject as a result of writing about it?

4. Which exploration techniques work best for you?

5. Do you use outlines? If so, what purpose do they serve?

6. Do you make changes in your writing as you go along, or do you write an entire draft without stopping?

7. Do you ever stop and wonder if your ideas will get through to your reader?

8. How many drafts do you usually write?

9. Do you show drafts of papers to anyone?

10. What is your usual reaction to early drafts of your papers?

11. Do you think about a reader when you are writing?

12. What do you do to come up with new words?

13. Have you ever thrown away an entire draft of a paper and started over again?

14. How do you find out if your ideas are getting through to your reader?

15. What part of a paper do you find most difficult to write?

16. Which kinds of papers do you prefer to write—those based solely on your own experience or those that require you to expand your viewpoint?

17. What changes have you made in your writing habits? What changes might you make?

Group Activity 3   With the whole class or in a small group, share your responses to the above writer's inventory. In listening to others' responses, you are likely to discover approaches to writing that are different from yours. Discussing with your classmates the problems writers face can give insight into your own writing process.

Study Entries: Reviewing Material from Other Courses

Your Writer's Notebook can be used to review material from other courses. The following kinds of entries are useful to reinforce what you are learning in other courses:

1. Prepare a one-page outline of your notes from a lecture, organizing the material into main points and supporting points.

2. Write an entry responding to an idea presented in a lecture in one of your courses. Begin by clearly stating the idea you wish to respond to. Show why this idea is important and how it relates to other ideas in that course.

3. Formulate a potential test question or an exam in another course and then write out an answer to that question.

On the next page are lecture notes from an astronomy class. Following the notes is an outline that organizes the notes.

Galaxies

new galaxies discovered due to technological
advances in astronomy; found in all directions of universe.
galaxies are groups of stars—millions to hundreds of billions
of stars. our sun—Milky Way Galaxy. (one of 17 in Local Group)
Galaxies are spiral or elliptical. MW has nucleus, disk, corona,
and spiral arms.
sun is part of a disk-shaped system and the Milky Way is the
light from the surrounding stars in the plane of the disk
 photographs of the MW taken by astronomers just show part
of the galaxy. galaxies throughout the universe (20 within 2 1/2
million LY; thousand within 50 million LY) separated by hundreds
of thousands to millions of LY. 1987: discovery of a new
galaxy in formation—12 billion light years away
from the earth.
called 3C 326.1 and is three times the
size of the Milky Way galaxy and is producing thousands of new
stars a year. This galaxy first discovered through radio waves
and then through optical telescopes.

**The material from these lecture notes is easier to review when it is
organized into an outline.**

Galaxies

   I.   Description
      A. Large groups of stars containing millions to hundreds of billions of
         stars.
      B. Most galaxies fall into two categories.
         1. Spiral
         2. Elliptical

  II. Number and distribution
      A. Galaxies extend in all directions to the limits of the observable
         universe
         1. 20 known galaxies within 2 1/2 million light-years.
         2. thousands of galaxies within 50 million light-years.
      B. Galaxies are separated by hundreds of thousands to millions of
         light-years

 III. Milky Way galaxy
      A. Milky Way is one of 17 galaxies in Local Group
      B. Milky Way is a spiral galaxy consisting of a nucleus, a disk, a
         corona, and spiral arms
      C. Our sun is a star in the disk-shaped system
         1. Milky Way is the light from the surrounding stars in the plane of
           the disk
         2. Photographs of the Milky Way taken by astronomers only show
           part of the galaxy

IV. Discovery of galaxy in formation
   A. Description
      1. Called 3C326.1
      2. Is 12 billion light-years from the earth
      3. Galaxy is three times the size of the Milky Way
      4. Producing thousands of new stars a year
   B. Implications of discovery
      1. Evidence of advance in technology (radio and optical telescopes)
      2. Discovery expands our knowledge about the limits and the formation of the universe

Writing Activity 14   Prepare a one-page outline of your notes from a lecture in another course, organizing the material into points and supporting points.

Writing Activity 15   Go back through your lecture notes from one of your other classes and select an idea to which you wish to respond. Write a short response in which you state the idea and then explain why it is important and how it relates to other ideas in that course.

Writing Activity 16   Plan a potential exam question that is likely to be asked in one of your classes. Then plan and write a response that clearly and completely answers the question.

Study Entries: Concept Lists

A concept list is composed of terms that represent important ideas in a class you are taking or a field you are studying. When you add a term to your concept list, don't simply copy the definition from a textbook or dictionary. Instead define the term as much as possible in your own words. Include examples to insure that you understand the concept. Try to relate the term to other concepts in the field.

Below are two entries from a concept list compiled for an introductory psychology class:

Introvert   This is a term first used by Carl Jung to describe a type of personality. An introvert tends to look inward toward himself and is more interested in ideas than in people. The opposite type is an extrovert who tends to look outward to the outside world and is more sociable. Most people cannot be classified exactly into one of these two categories.

Defense Mechanisms   These are techniques many people use to defend themselves in situations where their ego is threatened. Usually people use defense mechanisms without being aware of what they are doing because they do not want to honestly face up to a problem. An example of a defense mechanism is projection. In projection, we blame others for our own problems.

Writing Activity 17   Compile a list of the key concepts in one of your courses.

1. Identify terms that occur frequently in the textbooks, lectures, or outside reading in that course.
2. Using your own words as much as possible, write a definition for each term that helps you understand the concept to which that term refers. Include examples that illustrate the use of each term. Relate the terms to other concepts in the field.

Chapter 3
*Exploring Topics*_____

- ■ Exploration Techniques
      Brainstorming
      Clustering
      Discovery Writing

EXPLORATION TECHNIQUES_____

Keeping a Writer's Notebook allows you to practice writing on a regular basis and helps to prepare you for the more formal writing tasks (papers or reports) that are required in college or in your career. In Chapter 3, we present three techniques—brainstorming, clustering, and discovery writing—to use for exploring topics when you are writing papers and reports. After you have explored a topic using one or more of these techniques, you can then analyze and focus the material using the methods presented in Chapter 4.

Brainstorming

Brainstorming is simply a very free listing of words or phrases that occur to you as you think about the topic you are exploring. To begin a brainstorming list, start at the top of a fresh sheet of paper and list everything that comes to mind as you think about your topic. Don't restrain or edit your thinking, even if some of what you write down seems silly or irrelevant.

   Then as you start to run out of ideas, extend your list by asking *exploration questions* about your topic. Any question may help to extend a brainstorming list, but here are two sets of questions that often prove useful. The first set, sometimes referred to as the journalistic questions because of their use in newspaper writing, is easily remembered and may be applied to almost any topic.

   Who? (What persons are involved in the topic being explored?)

   What? (What actions, objects, or ideas are involved?)

   When? (What significant times or periods are involved?)

   Where? (What places are involved in the topic?)

Why? (What caused the actions involved in the topic?)

How? (In what manner or through what method were actions carried out?)

The following questions are somewhat more complex:

What can you *describe* about your topic?

What *changes* have occurred in it?

Can you relate an *incident* about it?

What do you *remember* about it?

What are its *parts, sections,* or *elements?*

Can you give *instructions* for making or doing it?

How do you *respond* to it or *feel* about it?

Why is it *valuable* or *important?*

What *causes* it? What *results* from it?

What can it be *compared* to?

Are you *for or against* it? Why?

The brainstorming list below was written about homeless people. Notice that it begins with the details and ideas that first occurred to the writer and that the list is then extended through the use of various exploration questions.

Homeless People

dirt, cold
bridges—sleep under
sick
mental illness
trash dumpster ⟹ Hungry
robbed
clothes in bags

taxes
life almost over
sidewalk
shelters
drunks, wine bottles in pockets
whole families
jobs—unemployment

Who?   mentally ill, unemployed, old people, young people some families

What?   being without shelter, or any security
hunger
no hope or dignity

When?   last few years; the Great Depression (30's)
always a problem, but worse recently

Where?   all over cities around here -- cities across the
nation. Rural areas?
streets, parks, churches, — or TV

Why?   good question. Economy? Fault of the homeless?
(Some politicians say this)
Attitude of society?

How?   through loss of jobs, evictions
divorce
some homeless people were once cared for in
mental hospitals — now roam streets.

Describe?   People sitting all day in library; men sleeping in
all-night donut shops; cardboard shelters under
freeway bridges; shopping carts with belongings;
men and women climbing through trash, look for
cans

Changes?   Getting worse. Winter now, and there seem to be
more people on the street. (Really bad back East.)
News coverage has increased.

Incident?   Man I gave ride to — but I really didn't believe
his story.

Instructions?   ??? Interesting: to become homeless, just lose money
and contact with family and friends. It's easy
to do, can happen easily.

Response? I feel sympathetic, but I don't do much. (That's probably the problem: feeling, but no action. How do we take action? What needs to be done? What _can_ be done?)

Importance? It just seems wrong. Some of the homeless may be responsible for what has happened to them, but is this true of most of them? We spend so much money on other things — why can't we help these people?

Reminders for Brainstorming

1. List everything that comes to mind and consider all the exploration questions, even if you don't respond to them all.
2. Don't ignore "crazy" ideas or details that seem insignificant. These may lead you to ideas that *are* important. (In the example above, notice how the detail about trash dumpsters helped to remind the writer of the much more important idea of hunger.)
3. Don't worry about being messy or disorganized. Brainstorming should not be a neat or mechanical procedure. The purpose of brainstorming is to *explore* a topic, not to produce a tidy list of the most common ideas about it.

Group Activity 1   *Brainstorming in a Group*

Brainstorming works well in groups, since there are more people to contribute ideas. Choose a topic that everyone in the group can agree upon, or use one provided by your instructor. Select one person to record the group's responses. (If possible, record the list on the blackboard where everyone can see it.) Then start brainstorming. After the group begins to run out of ideas, remember to use the exploration questions on pp. 26–27 to extend the list.

Here are several possible brainstorming topics:

What success means to me

Problems in education

Changes in family life today

Changes in the way men and women relate

Drugs and society

Writing Activity 1   *Making a Brainstorming List*

Brainstorm a topic you have selected or one provided by your instructor. As you make your list, try to move quickly from one idea to the next without worrying about being messy or about putting down thoughts that don't seem important. Remember to use the exploration questions once you start to run out of ideas.

Here are some brainstorming topics to consider:

What irritates me

Changes I'd like to make in my life

Heroes

Family traditions

Clustering

Like brainstorming, clustering lets you quickly record your ideas about a topic. Clustering, however, also permits you to show the *connections* between these ideas. For this reason some people find that clustering results in a better map of their thoughts about a topic.

To begin clustering, put your topic idea down in the middle (not the top) of a piece of paper and draw a small circle around it.

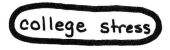

Then begin thinking about the topic, recording details and ideas in other circles connected to the first one.

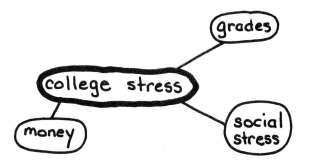

After you do this for a time, you'll find yourself branching out, connecting ideas not to the original circle but to later ones. This is fine—in clustering you want to generate a map that indicates how your ideas about a topic are connected.

When you begin to run out of ideas, use the exploration questions to extend your thinking, connecting your responses to the relevant parts of the cluster.

Exploration Questions

Who? (What persons are involved?)

What? (What actions, objects, or ideas are involved?)

When? (What significant times or periods are involved?)

Where? (What places are involved?)

Why? (What caused the actions involved in the topic?)

How? (In what manner or through what method were actions carried out?)

What can you *describe* about your topic?

What *changes* have occurred in it?

Can you relate an *incident* about it?

What do you *remember* about it?

What are its *parts, sections, or elements*?

Can you give *instructions* for making or doing it?

How do you *respond* to it or *feel* about it?

Why is it *valuable* or *important*?

What *causes* it? What *results* from it?

What can it be *compared* to?

Are you *for or against* it? Why?

Example

Here is the example cluster after it was extended through the use of exploration questions.

Reminders for Clustering

1. **As with brainstorming, don't be afraid to put down odd ideas or details that seem unimportant, and don't worry about being messy; clustering almost demands it.**
2. **As you construct a cluster, consider how an idea in one part of the cluster relates to ideas on other branches of the cluster. This is a good way to come up with new thoughts about your topic.**

Writing Activity 2   *Making a Cluster*

Make a cluster on a topic that you have selected or one that has been provided by your instructor. As you cluster, record details and ideas quickly and in a way that shows how they are connected. Remember to use the exploration questions on pp. 26–27 when you begin to run out of ideas.

Here are some topics to consider for a cluster:

A favorite activity or place

Why people fight

Your opinions on a political issue (local or national)

The qualities of a friend

Five improvements you might make as a student

Discovery Writing

Like brainstorming and clustering, discovery writing represents a time in the writing process when you are still exploring your topic to find out what you want to say about it. Discovery writing is simply a focused kind of freewriting. It lets you generate ideas for a paper at the same time you develop a feel for the paper's form. Some writers use a series of discovery writings as they work toward what they want to say in the final version of the paper.

There is no trick to writing discovery drafts; simply focus your attention on the topic, relax, and free write. As you find yourself running out of ideas, use the same exploration questions that you used in brainstorming and clustering:

Who?   (What persons are involved?)

What?   (What actions, objects, or ideas are involved?)

When?   (What significant times or periods are involved?)

Where?   (What places are involved?)

Why?   (What caused the actions?)

How? (In what manner or through what method were actions carried out?)

What can you *describe* about your topic?

What *changes* have occurred in it?

Can you relate an *incident* about it?

What do you *remember* about it?

What are its *parts, sections, or elements?*

Can you give *instructions* for making or doing it?

How do you *respond* to it or *feel* about it?

Why is it *valuable* or *important?*

What *causes* it? What *results* from it?

What can it be *compared* to?

Are you *for or against* it? Why?

Example

The following discovery writing deals with environmental problems:

When I think of environmental problems, I mainly think of pollution— air pollution, water pollution. Around here the main environmental problem that I am aware of is toxic chemicals in the wells. Every week or two it seems they discover a new well that has to be shut down because it has been polluted with cancer-causing chemicals. (Actually, smog is the biggest pollution problem around here, since it happens almost every day, but the water problem is perhaps even more serious, since cancer can kill you.) What worries me is how the problem can be stopped when it is almost impossible to identify the people who cause it. A truck dumps a load of chemicals in the middle of the night and years later the chemicals enter a well—how can you trace that?

Another environmental problem doesn't have to do with pollution—it's just overcrowding. The freeways are getting more crowded and people are now living in apartments and condos instead of houses, and the houses are getting smaller and packed closer together. All of this probably contributes to a lot of pollution, but even if the environment was kept clean, there would still be a problem. People get stressed when they can't get any privacy or quiet.

Who? Animals as well as people. What? Poisons. Also parts of the environment wear out—farmland gets played out and blows away in the wind. And another way to look at environmental problems is simply as overcrowding, which leads to poisoning and wearing out the environment. Is overcrowding the key? When? Well, now, especially, or at least environmental problems seem to be getting worse since I was born. Where? Everywhere, even the South Pole. (An article in the newspaper last week described a big hole in the upper atmosphere above the South Pole that lets in cosmic rays. The protective layer against these rays is breaking down because of air pollution. And the temperature is rising.) Why? Right now I'm thinking of overcrowding as the key, but perhaps there are other reasons.

Describe? One of the problems is that you can't see a lot of environmental problems—water pollution, nuclear radiation, toxic chemicals in food. Changes? Things seem to be getting worse, although more people are starting to pay attention. Incident? Well, even though I'm affected by it, I haven't been involved in any actual incidents. It's more of a day-to-day thing that involves everybody. But last year I was in a huge traffic jam when a freeway was closed while the fire department washed down a chemical spill. Those kinds of incidents happen often. Parts? That's one of the things that make the topic scary—there are so many ways that the environment is being damaged. Instructions? That's frightening too—it's pretty easy to give instructions for damaging the environment. Some hair sprays damage the atmosphere. Even using water around here can cause damage somewhere else, where the water came from. Driving your car contributes to smog. Feel? I worry about it when I think about it, but that isn't very often. Important? Yes, it's very important, even though it doesn't get the headlines some other issues do. Causes? Possibly overcrowding and neglect or poor planning. Plus some people are simply selfish in making messes that cause problems for other people to clean up or live with. Compared to? In a way, environmental problems are like cancer—we may not notice them until it's too late to do much about it. For or against? I'm against them, of course, but I'm not doing much to prevent environmental problems.

Reminders for Discovery Writing

Remember, discovery writing is not polished or final. Be as messy as you please and let your thoughts go where they will. Don't worry about grammar or spelling errors, since this may prevent you from freely exploring your topic.

Writing Activity 3   *Doing Discovery Writing*

Select a topic you are interested in or use one assigned by your instructor. Write freely about this topic until you begin to run out of ideas; then use the exploration questions to extend your discovery writing.

Here are some topics that you might use to practice discovery writing:

Prejudice

A challenging or dangerous activity

A person I admire

Irritating habits

A job I'll never forget

Chapter 4
From Exploratory Writing to Paper: Focusing and Ordering Your Material ___

- Strategy 1: Begin to Focus Your Paper by Limiting the Topic You Are Exploring
- Strategy 2: Decide What Point You Want to Make About Your Topic
    - Constructing a Main Point
    - Revising a Main Point
- Strategy 3: Prepare a Rough Plan of How You Will Develop Your Paper
- Strategy 4: Write Your Paper, Using Your Rough Plan As A Guide

In the preceding chapter, you studied a number of exploration techniques that you can use to generate ideas and details about topics. What do you do with the material generated by these techniques? How do you move from this material—clusters, brainstorming lists, and discovery writing—to a more focused, structured piece of writing?

In exploring a topic, you will accumulate more material than you can use. In this sense, you face the same dilemma that a photographer faces in taking a picture: you can't look at, frame, and record everything at once. At some point, you must survey a large field of material and then focus on one part of your material.

Making sense of your exploration writing is not going to be neat, orderly, or predictable. In order to move from this exploration writing to a paper, you will usually need to use the following strategies.

Strategy 1: Begin to focus your paper by limiting the topic you are exploring.

Strategy 2: Decide what point you want to make about your topic.

Strategy 3: Prepare a rough plan of how you will develop your paper.

Strategy 4: Write your paper, using your rough plan as a guide.

In the rest of this chapter, you will see the path one writer took from an exploratory cluster to a finished piece of writing.

If you plan to go through the process of writing a paper as you work through Chapter 4, you will need to complete all of the writing activities.

STRATEGY 1: BEGIN TO FOCUS YOUR PAPER BY LIMITING THE TOPIC YOU ARE EXPLORING

The process of focusing your paper is difficult because it's messy and unpredictable, and much of it takes place inside your head. Therefore, it is often valuable to talk through paper ideas in conferences and reading groups. In focusing your paper, use the guidelines below.

1. Begin to focus by finding some part of your material that holds a strong interest for you. Identify and mark other parts of the cluster, brainstorming list, or discovery writing related to the focus you have chosen.

2. Consider different kinds of papers that could evolve from your cluster, brainstorming list, or discovery writing. Look for connections or patterns in your material that suggest a possible paper. The paper options suggested below can be useful in helping you to determine the *kind* of paper you want to write.

Paper Options

a. Show how one event, problem, situation, or action leads to a number of results.

b. Explain what factors cause(d) something to be the way it is.

c. Describe how something has changed or how it should be changed.

d. List and describe the major qualities or characteristics of something.

e. Show step-by-step how something is done.

f. Compare or contrast two things.

g. Write about a person or persons central to an issue.

h. Divide something into its major parts.

i. Make an important point about a significant incident.

Keeping Healthy

3. After finding some part of your material that holds a strong interest for you and after considering your paper options, decide what you will focus on.

4. After selecting a focus, you may need to further explore that topic in another cluster, brainstorming list, or discovery writing.

Below are examples of kinds of papers that might come from the cluster on the opposite page: "Keeping Healthy."

Find some part of your cluster that holds a strong interest for you.

1. One of the parts of the cluster that interested this writer was *Sports and keeping healthy.* The gray shading shows other parts of the cluster that are related to this interest.

Consider different kinds of papers that could evolve from your material.

2. The writer looked through the options listed above and came up with the following ideas.

   a. Show how one event, problem, situation, or action leads to a number of results.

   Paper idea: Describe how improper aerobics instruction can lead to serious injuries.

   b. Explain what factors caused something to be the way it is.

   Paper idea: List and describe pressures that lead certain athletes to take steroids.

   c. Show how something should be changed.

   Paper idea: Present a detailed plan for developing eating habits better suited to athletic training.

   d. List and describe the major characteristics or qualities of something.

   Paper idea: Detail the common myths about what athletes should eat when in training.

   e. Show step-by-step how something is done.

   Paper idea: Describe a good exercise workout for an older person.

Decide what you want to focus on in your paper.

3. The writer considered the ideas above and decided to write a paper on common myths about what athletes should eat while in training.

Group Activity 1   *Consider Your Paper Options and Find a Strong Focus*

In small groups or as a class, look back at the cluster "Keeping Healthy" and consider what other ideas might come from it. Respond to each task that follows.

1. Find some part of the cluster that holds a strong interest for you. Identify or mark other parts that are related to this interest.

_____

_____

2. Consider different kinds of papers that could evolve from the cluster. Use the suggestions below to help you.

    a. Show how one event, problem, situation, or action leads to a number of results.

       Paper idea: _____

       _____

    b. Describe what factors caused something to be the way it is.

       Paper idea: _____

       _____

    c. Explain how something has changed or how it should be changed.

       Paper idea: _____

       _____

    d. List and describe the major qualities or characteristics of something.

       Paper idea: _____

       _____

    e. Compare or contrast two things.

       Paper idea: _____

       _____

    f. Describe a person or persons central to an issue.

       Paper idea: _____

       _____

    g. Divide something into its major parts.

       Paper idea: _____

       _____

    h. Show step-by-step how something is done.

       Paper idea: _____

       _____

    i. Make an important point about a significant incident.

       Paper idea: _____

       _____

Writing Activity 1   *Consider Your Options and Find a Strong Focus*

Select a cluster, brainstorming list, or discovery writing that you would like to continue to work with. Respond to each task below.

1. Find part of the cluster that holds a strong interest for you. Mark other parts of the cluster that are related to this interest.

   _____

   _____

2. Consider different kinds of papers that could evolve from the cluster. Use the suggestions below to help you.

   a. Show how one event, problem, situation, or action leads to a number of results.

      Paper idea: _____

      _____

   b. Describe what factors caused something to be the way it is.

      Paper idea: _____

      _____

   c. Explain how something has changed or how it should be changed.

      Paper idea: _____

      _____

   d. List and describe the major qualities or characteristics of something.

      Paper idea: _____

      _____

   e. Compare or contrast two things.

      Paper idea: _____

      _____

   f. Describe a person or persons central to an issue.

      Paper idea: _____

      _____

   g. Divide something into its major parts.

      Paper idea: _____

      _____

h. Show step-by-step how something is done.

Paper idea: _____

_____

i. Make an important point about a significant incident.

Paper idea: _____

_____

3. After finding some part of your material that holds a strong interest for you and after considering your paper options, decide what you will focus on in your paper._____

_____

4. Consider doing a second cluster, brainstorming list, or discovery writing that helps you further explore your more focused topic.

5. With another person—a student or your instructor—look over your responses to #2 above. Discussing your paper ideas with another person may help you pull together your options.

STRATEGY 2: DECIDE WHAT POINT YOU WANT TO MAKE ABOUT YOUR TOPIC

Constructing a Main Point

The *main point* or *thesis* of a paper is a statement that guides and controls that paper. The main point comes from your personal slant on the topic.

Regardless of when and how you do it, you must arrive at a main point before completing the final draft of a paper. That point will act as the controlling, guiding force in your paper. In most academic and business writing, you will state your main point directly, usually near the beginning of the paper, but not necessarily in the first sentence. Even if you write a paper in which the main point is not directly stated, you still need to know what that point is.

The main point you wish to make in a paper usually has to be shaped and refined during the writing process. Sometimes you will discover what point you want to make about your topic early in the exploration process. More often than not, you will need to settle on a working main point and then shape and refine it as you work on your paper.

Example: Working from a Cluster to a Main Point
On page 44 is a summary of how one writer moved from a cluster to a main point concerning myths about what athletes should eat while in training. The writer used the cluster on the opposite page (repeated from p. 38).

Keeping Healthy

1. The writer looked at the cluster and began to focus on part of the material that interested him. He chose *sports and keeping healthy* (circled with a dark line).

2. He then chose other parts of the cluster that related to *sports and keeping healthy* (see the gray shading in the cluster).

3. The writer next looked carefully at the connections he had marked in the cluster (gray shading) and thought of different kinds of papers that could come from that material. He decided that he would write on myths about what athletes should eat while in training.

4. The writer then went back to the cluster and circled with a dark line just the parts of the cluster that relate to myths about what athletes should eat while in training. He asked himself what statement he could make that would pull together all the parts of the cluster.

5. He came up with the following main point:

   By making careful choices, athletes can easily get the proteins, vitamins and minerals they need and thus avoid being victimized by dietary myths.

Using a Guide Sentence to Construct a Main Point. If you are having difficulty constructing a main point, try using the following guide sentence. Just complete this statement:

In my paper, I am trying to convince or show the reader that _____

_____

_____

(Of course, if you use the completed statement in your paper, you will drop the words, "In my paper I am trying to convince or show the reader that . . .")

Example: Using a Guide Sentence to Construct a Main Point
The writer who chose to focus on *myths about what athletes should eat while in training* would complete the statement like this:

In my paper, I am trying to convince or show the reader that *by making careful choices, athletes can easily get the proteins, vitamins and minerals they need and thus avoid being victimized by dietary myths.*

As the paper develops, the writer may continue to shape and refine this main point.

Exercise   *Constructing a Main Point*

Construct a clear, concise main point for each of these paper ideas from the cluster "Keeping Healthy."

> *Example:*   *Paper option:* Describe a person central to an issue.
>
> *Paper idea:* To use my grandmother as proof that older people can stay fit into their eighties.
>
> *Main point:* In my paper, I am trying to convince or show the reader that my eighty-year-old grandmother, who just walked ten miles in a walkathon, is living proof that people can stay fit much longer than we think.

1. Show how improper aerobics instruction can lead to serious physical injury.

   Main point: In my paper, I am trying to convince or show the reader that _____

   _____

   _____

2. Present a detailed plan for developing eating habits better suited to athletic training.

   Main point: In my paper, I am trying to convince or show the reader that _____

   _____

   _____

3. Detail a sensible exercise program for an older person.

   Main point: In my paper, I am trying to convince or show the reader that _____

   _____

   _____

4. Explain why the popular exercise myth "no pain, no gain" is so dangerous.

   Main point: In my paper, I am trying to convince or show the reader that _____

   _____

   _____

5. Compare the exercise clothing of a serious athlete to that of a person who joins a health club just for fun.

   Main point: In my paper, I am trying to convince or show the reader

   that _____

   _____

   _____

Writing Activity 2   *Constructing a Main Point or Thesis for Your Paper*

Go back to the paper ideas you developed in Writing Activity 1 on pages 41–42. Construct a working main point or thesis for each idea. Use the guide sentence below:

   In this paper, I am trying to convince or show the reader that _____

   _____

   _____

Save these main points for a later exercise.

Revising a Main Point

You may have difficulty focusing a paper if your main point is either too broad or too narrow.

1. A main point is *too broad* when it doesn't control or guide your writing. Consider this point taken from the cluster "Keeping Healthy."

   Broad main point: Health clubs are popular all over the country.

   A writer using this as a main point would be faced with showing the popularity of health clubs all over the United States, state by state— a book-length task. The writer could rework the main point so that it is more manageable:

   Revision: A number of factors have contributed to the increased popularity of health clubs in my community.

2. A main point that is *too narrow* does not leave the writer any room to develop the point. A statement of fact, for instance, does not need support. Consider this point:

   Narrow main point: My friend Julie has bulimia.

The writer has no place to go with such a main point because it is just a statement of fact.

Revision: Julie's bulimia is causing significant problems in her life.

This main point gives the writer an idea to support.

Group Activity 2   *Shaping and Refining a Main Point*

Read each main point below. After each one, indicate with an X whether the point is *too broad, too narrow,* or *OK.*

	Broad	Narrow	OK
Aerobic exercises done improperly may result in physical injury.	_____	_____	_____
We should all keep healthy.	_____	_____	_____
My friend Sally's life is completely dominated by her exercise mania.	_____	_____	_____
I exercise at the YMCA every Wednesday.	_____	_____	_____
With careful planning a student can have a healthful diet that is also low in cost.	_____	_____	_____
Much more research should be done on the use of vitamins.	_____	_____	_____
Ads for diet products and diet programs often make unrealistic claims about their results.	_____	_____	_____
My bad eating habits are causing me health problems.	_____	_____	_____
Marathons are held all over the country.	_____	_____	_____
My friend Mark is entering an Ironman competition.	_____	_____	_____

STRATEGY 3: PREPARE A ROUGH PLAN OF HOW YOU WILL DEVELOP YOUR PAPER

A rough plan is a short sketch in which you work out the way you will develop your paper. It serves as a guide to follow when you write. A rough plan contains the following.

1. The main point of your paper
2. The ideas you will use to support your main point arranged in the order you will present them

Below are a cluster and a rough plan developed from that cluster. Note that the writer focused on *the athlete's need to supplement his or her diet* and decided to explore that interest in a second cluster to get more detail.

Main point: By making careful food choices, athletes can easily get the proteins, vitamins, and minerals they need and thus avoid being victimized by dietary myths.

1. Myth that athletes need more protein

    Proteins are necessary, but excess proteins turn to stored fat.

    Fats don't convert to more power.

    The body naturally regulates amount of protein needed.

    Too much protein can lead to dehydration.

2. Myth that carbohydrate loading can give an athlete an extra boost during performance

    Athletes exercise heavily and eat lots of protein and fat.

    Then they cut down on exercise and load carbohydrates.

    Muscles are tricked into storing excess carbohydrate energy.

    This is dangerous—has side effects.

3. Myth that large doses of vitamins and minerals help the athlete

    Overdoses cause problems.

4. Well-balanced diet leads to best performance.

Writing Activity 3   *Developing a Rough Plan*

In Writing Activity 2, on page 46, you constructed several main points for your paper ideas. Select *one* of those main points that you would like to use for a paper. Work out a rough plan, showing how you might develop that paper.

STRATEGY 4: WRITE YOUR PAPER, USING YOUR ROUGH PLAN AS A GUIDE

Once you have developed a rough plan, use it as a guide when you start writing. Work through the plan by developing each major idea in your rough outline. Remember, you may think of additional ideas or details that you want to include. You may also want to change the order of your ideas. You may need to write several drafts of the paper before you are satisfied.

In Chapters 5, 6, and 8, we will be discussing in more detail the processes of OUTLINING, ORDERING YOUR MATERIAL, SUPPORTING YOUR MAIN POINT, AND REVISING YOUR WRITING.

The paper on pp. 50–51 was written from the rough plan on page 49. Although the writer wrote several earlier drafts, only the final draft is included here.

Dietary Myths of the Athlete
Michael O'Neill

My interest in nutrition and sports began when I left a desk job and a life of being overweight to return to college. One of the first courses I chose to enroll in was "Food and Nutrition: Concepts and Controversies." At the same time, I attended the college's Human Performance Laboratory to condition my body. Through these experiences, I became interested in exercise and nutrition. More specifically, I became interested in what athletes need to eat to keep in shape. Through the lab and the class, I found that many athletes are concerned about nutrition but are choosing diets and popping vitamins without much guidance. What they don't know is that by making careful food choices, they can easily get the proteins, vitamins, and minerals they need and thus avoid being victimized by dietary myths.

For example, one common myth believed by athletes is that they have a greater need for protein than nonathletes. This misconception is based on the fact that protein's major function in the body is to build and maintain muscle tissue. What athletes have not been told is that the body can use only so many proteins to make muscle tissue and the extra proteins are converted to fat and stored.

Although fat serves many important functions in the athlete's body such as lubricating joints and cushioning organs, extra fat does not contribute to strength or endurance; in fact, the overconsumption of protein has many health risks; one is dehydration. Dehydration can occur because water is used to carry the wasted protein out of the body. The athlete should be especially careful about this because water balance is of great importance to his performance.

Athletes do use a little more protein than nonathletes, but there is a margin of safety built into the protein recommendation for all people. This margin is high enough to cover the athlete's need.

Another myth believed by many athletes is that a technique called carbohydrate loading can be used without risk. Some athletes who compete in endurance events fool the muscles into storing extra carbohydrates with this technique. For several days they eat foods high in protein and fat and then exercise heavily. Then, they suddenly switch to a high carbohydrate diet and decrease exercise. This technique causes the muscles to store as much as four times their normal amount and so causes longer lasting energy.

Carbohydrate loading can have serious side effects. For instance it can cause abnormal heartbeat; swollen, painful muscles; and weight gain. The athlete should seriously consider the long-term effects of carbohydrate loading to determine if the risk is worth the benefit.

Still one other popular myth held by the athlete is that the use of megadoses of vitamins and minerals will improve performance. The old idea that if a little is good, a lot is better is being used here. The athlete should know that overdoses of vitamins and minerals are possible and they can cause many different problems. Vitamin A in capsule form, for example, is so toxic that it has been known to cause problems such as joint pain, stunted growth, bone abnormalities, nausea, and stomach and intestinal problems.

Based on what I have learned in my classes and in the lab, using vitamin and mineral supplements will not improve the performance of athletes unless they already have a deficiency. Since adequate vitamins and minerals are available in a well-balanced diet, athletes will get what they need by watching what they eat.

I've discussed only three of the many myths that are linked to the athlete and his diet. If similar myths could be covered here, the outcome would be the same. A normal, varied, well-balanced diet with some additional calories for increased energy use is what the athlete needs for strong performance.

Writing Activity 4   *Write Your Paper, Using Your Rough Plan As a Guide*

Using the rough plan you developed on page 49, write a paper that covers each of the parts of your plan. You may need to write several drafts before you feel that the paper is finished.

Chapter 5
Shaping and Arranging Ideas

- Ordering Strategies
    - General to Specific
    - Specific to General
    - Emphatic
    - Chronological Order
    - Causes/Effect
    - Cause/Effects
    - Comparison/Contrast
    - Change
    - Parts/Whole
- Using the Cause/Effects Ordering Strategy
- Mixing Ordering Strategies
- Outlining

In Chapter 4 you learned how to use a rough plan to order your ideas. In this chapter, you will look more closely at organization by exploring different patterns for arranging the ideas that go into your paper. You will also learn how to write an outline, which is an expanded version of a rough plan.

The way you arrange the material in your paper will depend on the kind of paper you are writing, the point you are making, and the way you want to order the support for that point. As you work out the order for your paper, remember that arrangement and rearrangement occur continually from rough plan to final draft.

ORDERING STRATEGIES

Certain patterns of order are part of our way of making sense of the world. These patterns allow us to sort out and organize ideas, facts, and details. We use these ordering strategies constantly when we think and write. Each of these patterns is based on a specific ordering principle.

Ordering Strategy   *Ordering Principle*

The first three ordering strategies are particularly important, since they come into play in almost all other types of ordering.

1. General to specific	Ordering from a general point or idea to specific support
2. Specific to general	Ordering from specific details, facts, examples, to a general point
3. Emphatic	Ordering from least important to most important
4. Chronological	Ordering by time and sequence (beginning-to-end order)

The following are other useful ordering strategies that may incorporate the strategies above.

5. Causes/effect	Ordering from several causes to one effect or result
6. Cause/effects	Ordering from one cause to several effects or results
7. Comparison/contrast	Ordering by showing similarities and differences
8. Change	Ordering by showing change
9. Parts/Whole	Ordering by showing the relationship of parts to whole

To illustrate each type of order, we have drawn from the cluster that was used at the beginning of Chapter 4 and is reproduced on the next page.

Keeping Healthy

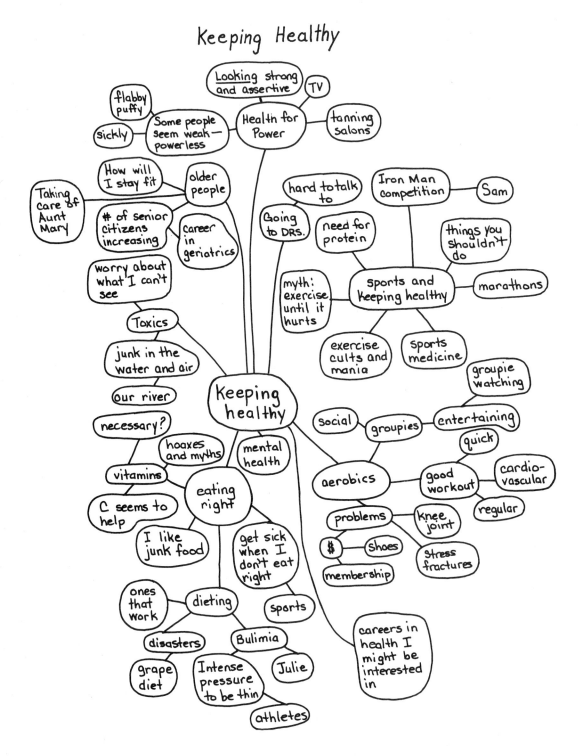

General to Specific

In general-to-specific arrangement, you move from a general idea to specific points that support that general idea. When you use this ordering strategy, ask these questions:

What details or ideas can I use to prove my point?

What examples could support what I am trying to say?

You will also find that you use general-to-specific order as part of most other ordering strategies.

Rough Plan

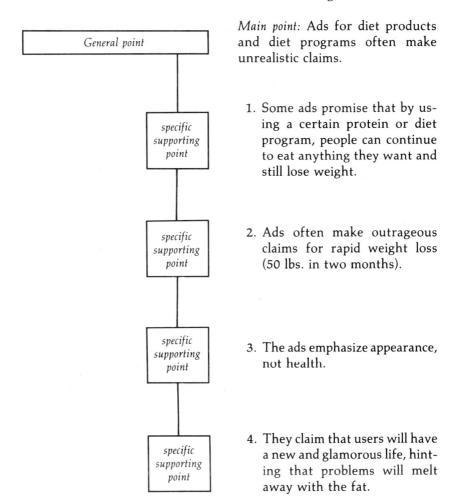

Main point: Ads for diet products and diet programs often make unrealistic claims.

1. Some ads promise that by using a certain protein or diet program, people can continue to eat anything they want and still lose weight.

2. Ads often make outrageous claims for rapid weight loss (50 lbs. in two months).

3. The ads emphasize appearance, not health.

4. They claim that users will have a new and glamorous life, hinting that problems will melt away with the fat.

Specific to General

When you use specific-to-general order, you lead up to your main point through a series of smaller points and answer questions like these:

What do these specific ideas and details add up to?

What point do they make?

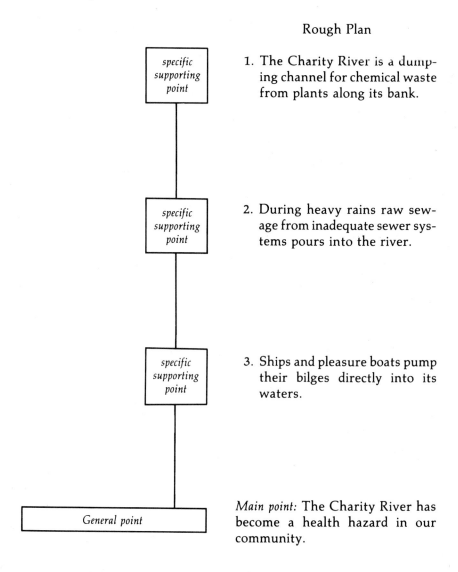

Rough Plan

specific supporting point

1. The Charity River is a dumping channel for chemical waste from plants along its bank.

specific supporting point

2. During heavy rains raw sewage from inadequate sewer systems pours into the river.

specific supporting point

3. Ships and pleasure boats pump their bilges directly into its waters.

General point

Main point: The Charity River has become a health hazard in our community.

Emphatic

When using emphatic order, you arrange ideas from least important to most important. By ending a piece of writing with your strongest point of evidence, you fix your point in the reader's mind. When you use emphatic order, ask these questions:

Which point is most important to me?

Which point will leave my reader with the strongest possible impression?

Emphatic order is frequently used in conjunction with other types of order.

Rough Plan

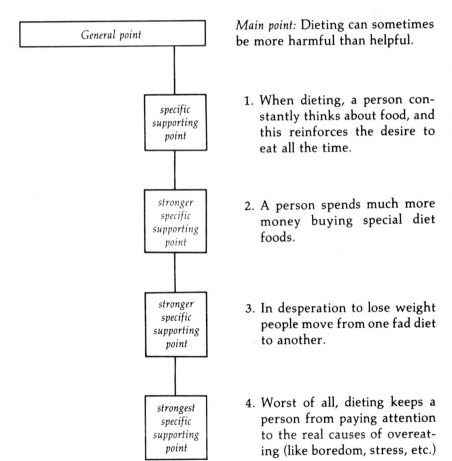

Main point: Dieting can sometimes be more harmful than helpful.

1. When dieting, a person constantly thinks about food, and this reinforces the desire to eat all the time.

2. A person spends much more money buying special diet foods.

3. In desperation to lose weight people move from one fad diet to another.

4. Worst of all, dieting keeps a person from paying attention to the real causes of overeating (like boredom, stress, etc.)

Chronological Order

Chronological order is time or beginning-to-end order. When you order chronologically, you answer these kinds of questions.

How did _____ happen?

What are the steps involved in _____ ?

How is _____ done?

Rough Plan

General point

first event

second event

third event

fourth event

fifth event

Main point: A sequence of events led me to choose geriatric nursing as a career.

1. When my elderly aunt came to live with us, I enjoyed being with her and taking care of her.
2. A test that measures aptitudes and interests indicated that I would be suited to and would enjoy nursing.
3. When my aunt entered a nursing home, I realized that I knew more about caring for older people than most of the nurses in the home.
4. When my aunt died, I missed the visits to the home and realized how much she and the home had become a part of my life.
5. At 45, I realized that I had the maturity, patience, skill, and dedication to work with the frail elderly.

Causes/Effect

If you are trying to show that many causes lead to one result, you answer questions such as:

If I do _____ , what will be the result?

What are the reasons for _____ ?

How did these causes lead to this result?

What will be the end result of these events, actions, or ideas?

Rough Plan

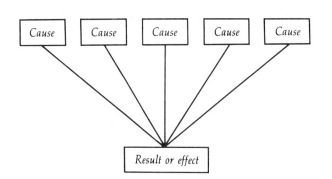

1. The waiting room is always packed with grouchy, impatient people.
2. The office help, including the nurses, are always abrupt and rude.
3. The doctor is always in a rush and seems irritated by my questions.
4. The doctor uses medical language that makes me feel that my body is a foreign object.
5. The doctor treats me like a child.

Main point: I am going to look carefully for a doctor who makes me feel more comfortable.

Cause/Effects

If you are showing that one cause leads to many results, answer these kinds of questions.

If I do _____, what will be the results?

What caused _____ to happen?

Rough Plan

Main point: The media's definition of healthy as slim, tan, well exercised, and vibrating with energy causes people to adopt dangerous health practices.

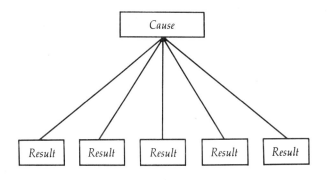

1. People develop eating disorders because they are desperate to stay slim.
2. People take vitamins and minerals in doses that are harmful, even toxic.
3. People bake themselves in the sun or in tanning salons to look healthy.
4. People caught up in the exercise craze often exercise beyond their limits or choose an inappropriate form of exercise that leads to injury.
5. People rely on drugs in an attempt to stay happy and alert.

Comparison/Contrast

When you compare and contrast, look for likenesses and differences between two objects, ideas, persons, etc. When you compare, ask questions like these:

How is _____ like _____?

How is _____ different from _____?

What aspects of _____ and _____ can be compared and contrasted?

There are two basic structures for ordering a piece of writing in which you compare and contrast two items.

1. *Block ordering:* In this structure, you discuss all the qualities and characteristics of the first item in the comparison/contrast pair. Then discuss the second item in the pair. Generally you use the same points of comparison and contrast to order your discussion of each of the two items.

2. *Alternating ordering:* In this structure, you move through the paper from one point of comparison to another. As you discuss a point, show first how it relates to one item in the comparison/contrast pair and then how it relates to the other.

Example: Block Ordering

Rough Plan

Main point

Main point: After doing some research on running and walking as forms of exercise, I have decided that walking is more appropriate for me.

Item #1

point of comparison
point of comparison
point of comparison
point of comparison

1. Running

Good cardiovascular exercise

Can be done quickly (20 minutes, four times a week)

Can lead to many physical injuries such as shin splints, knee problems

Hard to find suitable running partners

Item #2

point of comparison
point of comparison
point of comparison
point of comparison

2. Walking

   Good cardiovascular exercise

   Takes more time

   Low risk of injury

   Easier to find people to walk with

Example: Alternating Ordering

Rough Plan

Main point

Main point: After doing some research on running and walking as forms of exercise, I have decided that walking is more appropriate for me.

point of comparison

1. Cardiovascular effect

Item #1

   Running

Item #2

   Walking

point of comparison

2. Investment in time

Item #1

   Running

Item #2

   Walking

point of comparison

3. Risk of injury

Item #1

   Running

Item #2

   Walking

point of comparison

4. Finding people to exercise with

Item #1

   Running

Item #2

   Walking

Rough Plan

<u>Main point:</u> Strong mental health is not necessarily an inherited characteristic; most people have to work hard to maintain good mental health.

1. One must take responsibility for one's own life (including one's problems and actions) in order to feel more in control.

2. One needs to get plenty of rest.

3. One needs to eat sensibly.

4. One needs to find positive ways to handle stress.

5. One needs to face problems when they arise instead of ignoring them (problems at work with boss, disagreements with teachers, money problems).

6. One should consider seeking assistance from a qualified counselor or therapist when in need of help.

Outline

Main point: Good mental health is not necessarily an inherited trait; most people have to work hard to maintain a healthy mental outlook.

I. People need to take responsibility for their lives, including their mental health.

     A. People must admit that they <u>choose</u> to do the things they do.

         1. People often blame others for actions. ("My mother made me do it.")

         2. My neighbor blames her children when she gets mad and hits one of them.

     B. People will actually feel more in control when they see that all actions are a matter of personal choice.

II. People need to see that good mental health and good physical health are inseparable.

     A. Getting enough rest and eating properly.

         1. Certain foods can cause depression or anxiety (coffee, sugar—in excess).

         2. Drug use can lead to serious psychological problems.

     B. Certain health problems can lead to depression or anxiety. For example, I have a friend whose inner ear problems led to her tendency to withdraw from people.

III. People need to find positive ways to handle stress.

     A. Attend courses at hospital or college on handling stress.

         1. I learned to chart stress patterns.

         2. Learned simple meditation techniques.

     B. Find a relaxing form of exercise.

IV. People need to learn to face problems when they arise.

     A. Ignoring problems only leads to buildup of anger and frustration.

         1. Problems at home (family, money, house duties).

         2. Problems with teachers (I ignored comments on papers).

     B. Learn techniques for problem-solving process that involves identifying problem, finding creative solutions.

V. People should consider seeking assistance from a qualified therapist or counselor when problems seem out of hand.

     A. Many people think going to a therapist shows weakness.

     B. Neutral person can be more objective and can teach one strategies for dealing with problems.

     C. Family that came to speak to our psychology class about their family therapy experience.

Once you have written an outline, you don't have to follow it strictly when you write your paper. You can rearrange points and add or delete material.

Chapter 6
Strengthening Your Support

- The Need for Support
- Types of Support
- Levels of Support
- Language As Support
    Keeping a Vocabulary List
- Additional Work on Support: Analyzing Information and Essays

In preceding chapters, you learned techniques for exploring and focusing a topic and for constructing a main point or thesis about that topic. In order to convince your reader of your main point, you must have strong support for that point. In this chapter, you will learn how to strengthen your support by using detailed evidence and vivid language. With such support, you will be able to convince others of your point of view.

THE NEED FOR SUPPORT

In the paragraph below, the writer wants to convince her readers that working behind the lunch counter at Perry's was a difficult job.

Life Behind the Counter

Working behind the lunch counter at Perry's Five and Ten was the worst job I ever had. The work was exhausting and many of the customers were difficult to please. I tried hard to do everything right, but somehow I always came up short. Mr. Perry was a really difficult boss to work for. I hated his attitude towards his employees. I believe that he felt he could exploit us because we didn't have skills for any other job. Some parts of the job made me feel like Cinderella. The only thing that made the job bearable was the support I got from some of the other employees. It also helped to know that for me the job was temporary.

This paragraph has a general idea ("working behind the counter at Perry's Five and Ten was difficult"), but it offers few specific details to back up that general idea. The writer has not described the experience so that the reader can see it and share it.

Think of all the questions a reader is left with after reading "Life Behind the Counter":

☐ What exactly were the duties of the job?

☐ What did Mr. Perry do that made him such a difficult boss?

☐ What parts of the job made the writer feel like Cinderella?

☐ How specifically were the customers a problem?

☐ What kind of support did the writer get from the other employees?

☐ Why did the writer see the job as temporary?

In the following revision of "Life Behind the Counter," the support has been strengthened so that many of these questions are answered.

Life Behind the Counter

Always hot, always tired, always hurrying—that's what I remember about working as a grill cook and counter girl at the lunch counter at Perry's Five and Ten. I worked at Perry's for five months before I started college, and my job there was a difficult experience.

The job was exhausting. I started at 7:00 a.m. and didn't get off until after 3 p.m. During much of the day we had people standing in line waiting for seats, so we had to rush around taking and filling orders as fast as possible. Even during the lull before the lunch trade, we had dozens of chores such as filling salt and pepper shakers and chopping tomatoes. After the lunch counter closed, I had to clean the grill and mop the floor. I used to feel like Cinderella before she was rescued by Prince Charming as I wrung out the mop in a bucket of dirty water.

Some of the customers made the job harder. I hated people who came in with toddlers because they would let the children throw food, spill Cokes, and crumble packages of saltine crackers all over the floor. Other people would make disgusting messes by leaving soggy, balled-up napkins and empty catsup packages all over the counter and floor. People hardly ever tipped even when they made messes or demanded instant service. They treated me like a servant.

The worst thing about the job was the way I was treated by Mr. Perry, the owner. He was always watching to see if we did something wrong. That made me nervous and then I would add up a check wrong or drop an order on the floor. He was cheap and got angry when we broke something or if he thought we were wasting food. Once he yelled at me that I was using too much tuna fish when I made tuna sandwich platters. The employees stuck together against Mr. Perry, and sometimes when he wasn't there we joked around and imitated his whiny voice. Even though I liked the other people who worked there, I was overjoyed on the day I told Mr. Perry that I was quitting. I felt fortunate that I was able to leave. I knew the other women working the counter would probably not have that chance.

We now know much more about why the writer disliked working at Perry's. The specific details in the revised paragraph provide evidence to support the writer's contention that "working behind the counter at Perry's is difficult." Because the general statements from the first version have better support and the language has become more specific, the revised paragraph is more convincing.

TYPES OF SUPPORT

In trying to persuade your reader to see your point or share your perspective, use a *combination* of different kinds of evidence: details, facts, incidents, reasons, and examples. Choose support that will convince your reader of the point you are trying to make. Different kinds of ideas call for different types of support. A paper advocating gun control might use mostly facts and reasons; a personal account of the joys of white-water canoeing might rely mainly on incidents and details.

When you explore a topic, consider the many different kinds of evidence you can use. For example, if you were exploring the topic "Angel Community Park," you could use several different kinds of evidence:

1. *Descriptive details.* If your point were that "Angel Community Park was in poor condition before 1984," you could support that point with specific details:

   a. Broken bottles and trash littered the area.

   b. Graffiti covered the walls of the buildings.

   c. The playground equipment was falling apart.

   d. A fire burned off most of the plants and shrubs.

2. *Facts* (verifiable pieces of information). If you wanted to prove that "the city has made a sincere commitment to restore Angel Community Park," you could list these verifiable facts:

   a. The city spent $1 million in general restoration over a three-year period.

   b. A modern community center was added in 1985.

   c. Six tennis courts and three handball courts were built in 1986.

   d. All the buildings were repainted in 1987.

3. *Incidents* (actual events). If you wanted to show that "Angel Community Park needs more frequent patrol by the park officers," you could list these actual events:

   a. Many people let their dogs run free instead of using a leash, and last week a little boy was bitten on the leg.

    b. Teenagers gather in the parking lot on Friday and Saturday nights to drink and party; last weekend damage was done to park facilities after one of these late-night parties.

    c. There is still some gang activity in the park—two months ago there was a drive-by shooting.

4. *Reasons* (justifications or explanations). If you wanted to argue that "community members should be charged a fee for park use," you could explain or justify your position with the following reasons:

    a. The park cannot be maintained properly with city funds alone.

    b. People tend to appreciate something more if they're paying for it.

    c. The community center can be expanded and additional staff and facilities added.

5. *Examples* (instances or illustrations). If your point is that "Angel Community Park is heavily used by the people in the neighborhood," you could cite these examples:

    a. People picnic there every weekend during the summer.

    b. People of all ages play a variety of sports in the park, including tennis, baseball, softball, and handball.

    c. The after-school play program is used by the children of working parents.

    d. The community center offers a variety of classes and programs during the day and in the evening.

Remember, do not worry too much about identifying the *type* of support you use in your writing. What counts is that you provide clear and *adequate* support. These categories are listed only to remind you of the range and variety of support you can use in your writing.

Exercise 1   *Identifying Support*

Read the selection below carefully. Then complete the questions at the end.

Man Bites Man | *Patrick Huyghe*

An angry Detroit crowd of 40 people attacked and bit two emergency-service technicans last May because it took them so long to get to the scene of a traffic accident. A month earlier a traveling salesman was found guilty of biting off a woman's nose during an attack in a hotel parking lot in Norfolk, Virginia. And about a year ago James Garner, known to television viewers as private eye Jim Rockford, tried to bite the motorist who grabbed, beat, and choked him after a minor traffic accident in Los Angeles.

3. The house at the end of the block is an embarrassment to the whole neighborhood.

Support: _____

_____

_____

_____

4. The new shopping mall on the outskirts of town has caused a number of problems.

Support: _____

_____

_____

_____

5. Alcohol abuse causes serious problems for families and communities.

Support: _____

_____

_____

_____

Writing Activity 1   *Supporting a Point*

In each sentence below, complete the point by filling in the blank with a topic of your choice. Then develop a combination of details, facts, examples, incidents, and examples that could support the point about that topic.

Example

The Salvation Army _____ has made a valuable contribution to the community.

Support: *The army offers family counseling services. It runs a youth hostel for runaways. It operates a thrift shop where low-cost shoes and clothing can be purchased. It serves several hundred hot meals everyday at the downtown center. Last Christmas it collected new toys to give to families in need.*

1. I think _____ is the most disappointing holiday of the year.

   Support: _____

   _____

   _____

   _____

2. _____ is my most valuable possession.

   Support: _____

   _____

   _____

   _____

3. _____ has been an important role model for me.

   Support: _____

   _____

   _____

   _____

4. _____ is the most irritating person I know.

   Support: _____

   _____

   _____

   _____

5. _____ has not lived up to my expectations.

   Support: _____

   _____

   _____

   _____

6. _____ is a problem that this community must face.

   Support: _____

   _____

   _____

   _____

Writing Activity 2   *Identifying Support*

Find in a newspaper or magazine an article on a subject you are interested in. Using the original or a photocopy of the article, underline the facts, details, incidents, reasons, and examples used as support in the article. Then answer the following questions:

1. What is the main point of the article?
2. What are the three most convincing pieces of evidence used to support that point?

LEVELS OF SUPPORT

Effective writing usually requires several levels of support. The main point of a paper will be supported by several subpoints (the first level of support) and each of these subpoints will in turn be given more detailed (second-level) support through the use of specific facts, incidents, details, examples, or reasons. Sometimes second-level support will be developed with even more detailed (third-level) support.

The diagram on the facing page provides an idealized or simplified picture of how the levels of support might appear in a paper. This diagram helps to emphasize three important ideas about how support is used in a paper:

1. Notice that each of the major subpoints is backed up with second-level support. A major subpoint that does not receive second-level support is likely to be weak and unconvincing. Usually, each major subpoint is developed (through second- and third-level support) in a paragraph of its own.
2. Notice that all pieces of detailed, second- or third-level support are organized under a major subpoint. Detailed support that is not directly related to a subpoint is apt to be confusing.
3. Notice finally that not all pieces of second-level support are themselves backed up with third-level support. This is only natural: the writing process is not mechanical, and you as the writer will have to judge when second-level support needs further development. The important thing is to make sure that all major subpoints are supported and that all detailed support is clearly connected to a relevant subpoint.

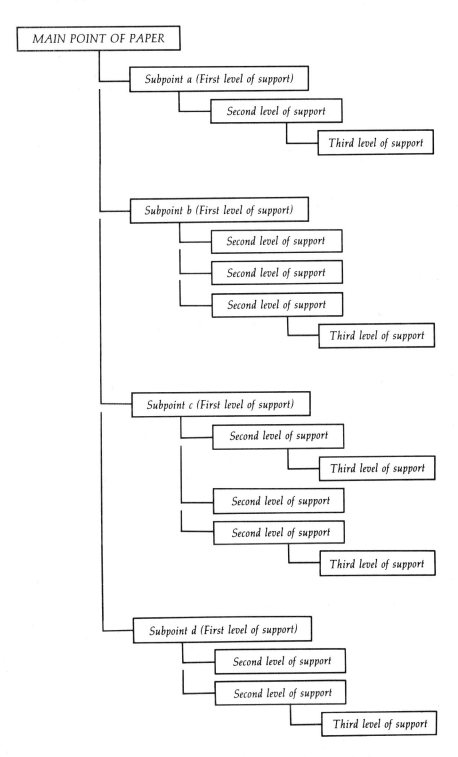

MAIN POINT OF PAPER

Subpoint a (First level of support)

Second level of support

Third level of support

Subpoint b (First level of support)

Second level of support

Second level of support

Second level of support

Third level of support

Subpoint c (First level of support)

Second level of support

Third level of support

Second level of support

Second level of support

Third level of support

Subpoint d (First level of support)

Second level of support

Second level of support

Third level of support

The following two diagrams analyze the support in "Life Behind the Counter" from p. 71. The first diagram shows the main point and the first-level support for the essay. This kind of diagram can help you check whether your subpoints provide logical support for your main idea.

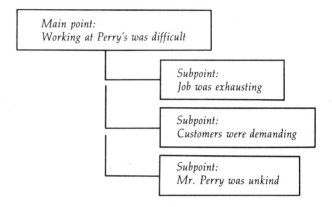

The second diagram analyzes the levels of support within the second paragraph of the essay. This kind of diagram can help you see whether a paragraph is logically supported and developed.

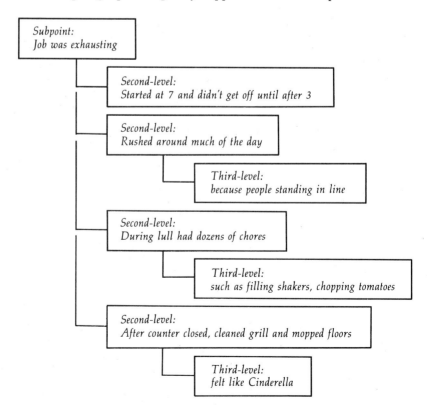

Exercise 2 *Analyzing Support Within a Paragraph*

Look carefully at the diagram on the bottom of page 80 showing the levels of support in the second paragraph of "Life Behind the Counter." Then construct your own diagram to show the levels of support in the third paragraph of that essay. When you finish, compare your diagram with that of a classmate.

Writing Activity 3 *Analyzing Support in a Paper*

1. Select a piece of writing to analyze. Your instructor may assign you an article or may ask you to work with one of your own papers.

2. Construct a diagram showing the levels of support in the piece of writing you have selected. Your diagram should show

   ☐ the main point
     ☐ all major subpoints (first level of support)
       ☐ the second-level support for each subpoint
         ☐ any items of third-level support

LANGUAGE AS SUPPORT

Making your writing stronger and more convincing does not necessarily mean using more words; it may simply mean using words that are more vivid or specific. Vivid, specific language enables your reader to share more fully in the ideas and experiences you are trying to communicate.

Exercise 3 *Analyzing Language*

Read the paper below, "Grandma's Hands," and underline any words that describe (1) how the grandmother's hands looked and (2) what she did with them.

Grandma's Hands | *Rene Milbery*

My most vivid memories of my grandma are of her hands. They were small, brown, wrinkled and plump. She had the softest touch as she gently combed out my long curly hair.

I remember how busy her hands were. Slap, slap, plop, roll; those were the sounds she would make while making tortillas. I would stand in the kitchen munching away on a soft, warm, buttery tortilla and watching in amazement as she worked with machine-like precision. Pinch the dough, slap, slap, plop down the dough on the flour-covered breadboard and roll. Then the tortilla went onto a hot griddle. She wouldn't stop until we had a large stack, enough to feed fifty family members.

Grandma never drove a car or worked a sewing machine. But she made the most beautiful baby blankets by hand. She would collect old clothes, old fabric squares, old baby blankets—and cut squares out of the colors she liked. Then she would sew them together by hand. Slowly she would create a beautiful, colorful blanket. My cousins would see a new baby wrapped in pieces of their past in those small squares.

Grandma was a woman of worldly wisdom. I'll never forget her lectures about getting too close to the "boys," or the terrible danger of having a child out of wedlock! Well, my seventeen-year-old cousin, Celia Anne, had a baby girl before Mother's Day, and she wasn't married! Celia Anne, or C-Anne as we called her, was so thin that she was able to conceal her pregnancy until a week before the baby's birth. The news shocked the family. We did not know about the baby until we heard that it had been born. C-Anne had a little girl, and the new mother and daughter came home from the hospital on the day before Mother's Day. So on Mother's Day we all gathered at my uncle's house to see C-Anne and the baby.

Most of the family members had already arrived. I will never forget the conversation we girl cousins had on the front lawn while waiting for Grandma and Grandpa to arrive.

My cousin Debbie said, "Boy, it's really gonna hit the fan when Grandma comes!"

"I know, I can hardly wait," I replied. Our adolescent minds reveled in each other's disasters.

"I was talking with C-Anne earlier," said Laura. "She's ashamed to see Grandma."

Sensing impending doom, I said, "Yeah, this is going to be great!"

Our conversation ended abruptly when Grandma's car entered the driveway. As was our custom, we all ran over to kiss Grandma. The family matriarch had arrived!

I remember leaning over to Debbie and saying, "Funny, she doesn't seem upset."

"I know," Debbie said disappointedly, "but let's follow her in anyway."

The other cousins remained outside, hoping to avoid an embarrassing situation. But Debbie and I weren't going to miss this for all the tea in China.

Grandma made her way through the crowd inside the house, through what seemed like endless hugs and kisses, and then started down the hall to C-Anne's room. My mother and C-Anne's mother were already there. Debbie and I were close behind Grandma. Much to our amazement, Grandma walked over to the bassinet, picked up the baby, and while lovingly holding the baby close to her with those soft, gentle hands, asked Celia Anne, "What are you going to name her?" C-Anne said, "Beatrice, after my mother."

I remember leaning over and whispering in Debbie's ear, "Boy, that was a political move!"

After those words were spoken, Grandma asked, "C-Anne, how are you feeling?"

C-Anne relaxed and said "Fine," and started telling Grandma all about her experience in the hospital. When she was finished, Grandma took the baby into the living room and played with her. Nothing more was said.

Needless to say, Debbie and I were in shock. Where were the hellfire and brimstone? This was a great example of true love and compassion. And I felt at that time just how much Grandma loved us. She taught us by example that day.

My grandma is gone now. I no longer have the slap, slap, plop, roll sounds coming from the kitchen. I no longer have the gentle touch of those small, brown, wrinkled hands gently combing my hair. But through her I have a strength and a sense of values that she instilled in me when I was small. And my youngest son, Trevor, sleeps on an old blanket that Grandma made for my babies. With these things, I feel that a piece of Grandma is still with me.

Review the words you have underlined and then respond to the following:

1. What are the most vivid words used in this piece?

   _____

   _____

2. What main point or points about the grandmother's character or significance are supported by the description of the hands?

   _____

   _____

Exercise 4   *Analyzing Language*

Professional writers use language that is specific and vivid. Edward Abbey, the contemporary nature writer, uses such language in *Desert Solitaire*, an account of a season he spent as a ranger in a remote national park in Utah. Read this excerpt from the book—on what has happened to Arches National Monument since he worked there—and then answer the questions below it.

Desert Solitaire | *Edward Abbey*

Arches National Monument has been developed. The Master Plan has been fulfilled. Where once a few adventurous people came on weekends to camp for a night or two and enjoy a taste of the primitive and remote, you will now find serpentine streams of baroque automobiles pouring in and out, all through the spring and summer, in numbers that would have seemed fantastic when I worked there, from 3,000 to 30,000 to 300,000 per year; the "visitation," as they call it, mounts ever upward. The little campgrounds where I used to putter around reading three-day-old newspapers full of lies and watermelon seeds have now been consolidated into one master campground that looks, during the busy season, like a suburban village; elaborate housetrailers of quilted aluminum crowd upon gigantic camper-trucks of Fiberglas and molded plastic; through their windows you will see the blue glow of television and hear the studio laughter of Los Angeles; knobby kneed oldsters in plaid Bermudas buzz up and down the quaintly curving asphalt road on motorbikes; quarrels break out between campsite neighbors while others gather around their charcoal briquettes (ground campfires no longer permitted—not enough wood) to compare electric toothbrushes. The Comfort Stations are there, too, all lit up with electricity, fully equipped inside, though the generators break down now and then and the lights go out, or the sewage backs up in the plumbing system (drain fields were laid out in sand over a solid bed of sandstone), and the water supply sometimes fails, since the 3000-foot well can only produce about 5 gpm—not always enough to meet the demand. Down at the beginning of the new road, at park headquarters, is the new entrance station and visitor center where admission fees are collected and where the rangers are going quietly nuts answering the same three basic questions five hundred times a day: (1) Where's the john? (2) How long's it take to see this place? (3) Where's the Coke machine?

Progress has come at last to the Arches, after a million years of neglect. Industrial Tourism has arrived.

1. What is the main point that Abbey is making in this passage?

   _____

   _____

   _____

2. Read through the selection again and underline the support for that point.

3. Identify the language that is particularly vivid and specific.

   _____

   _____

   _____

4. Look up in a dictionary any unfamiliar words from this excerpt. Add these words to your vocabulary list (see pp. 85).

Writing Activity 4   *Language As Support*

In a newspaper or magazine, find an article on a subject you are interested in. Using the original or a photocopy of the article, underline the words you find particularly specific and vivid. Then answer the following questions:

1. What is the main point of the article?

2. Of the words or phrases you found striking, which most effectively support the main point?

Keeping a Vocabulary List

Keeping a vocabulary list in your Writer's Notebook is a way to increase the number of words you understand and can use. Expanding your vocabulary will benefit both your writing skills and your critical thinking. As you improve your vocabulary, you increase your range and sophistication as a thinker.

The best words to put in your vocabulary list are those you *understand* as a reader but seldom *use* as a writer. When you come across such a word, write it in your notebook and then write a sentence of your own using the word.

If you are not completely sure of the meaning of a word, look it up in a dictionary. (A paperback dictionary is handy to carry around, but you should also consider investing in a desk edition of a college dictionary.) When you look up a word in a dictionary, read through the entire entry. Take note of the different meanings the word has. Check to see if the entry includes synonyms (different words with a similar meaning). Consider these two entries from *The American Heritage Dictionary:*

Note the range of meaning for *beguile.*

be·guile (bĭ-gīl′) *tr.v.* **-guiled, -guil·ing, -guiles. 1.** To deceive by guile; delude. **2.** To take away from by guile; cheat. **3.** To distract the attention of; divert. **4.** To pass (time) pleasantly. **5.** To amuse or charm; delight. **—be·guile′ment** *n.* **—be·guil′er** *n.*

Note the list of synonyms for *beg.* If you wanted to use one of these synonyms to replace *beg*, the definitions would help you pick the synonym with the precise meaning you needed.

beg (bĕg) *v.* **begged, beg·ging, begs.** *—tr.* **1.** To ask for as charity. **2.** To ask earnestly for or of; entreat. *—intr.* **1.** To solicit alms. **2.** To make a humble or urgent plea. **—*phrasal verb.* beg off.** To ask to be released from something, as an obligation. **—*idiom.* beg the question. 1.** To assume the conclusion to one's argument to be true. **2.** To equivocate or dodge an issue. [ME *beggen*, prob. < OFr. *begart*, beggar, ult. < MDu. *beggaert.*]

Synonyms: beg, crave, beseech, implore, entreat, importune. *Beg* and *crave* apply to the act of asking for something one cannot claim as a right, in a way that is earnest, humble, and designed to stir pity. *Beseech* emphasizes earnestness and implies great anxiety. *Implore* intensifies the senses of earnestness, humility, and anxiety. *Entreat* pertains to persuasive pleading calculated to overcome opposition. *Importune* adds the sense of persistent and sometimes harassing pleading.

Vocabulary List

beguile (v.)

1. to deceive

2. to charm

He used his charm and good looks to *beguile* her into reluctant agreement.

substantiate (v.)

1. to prove

2. to verify

The medical reports of malnutrition *substantiate* the claim that people are going hungry.

conscience (n.)

moral, ethical values

My *conscience* told me that I should not cheat on the test.

Writing Activity 5   *Keeping a Vocabulary List*

In your Writer's Notebook, label a page "Vocabulary List."

1. As you read, look for words that interest you and add them to your vocabulary list.

2. If you don't understand the word, look it up in a dictionary and add the definition beneath the word.

3. Using the word correctly, write a sentence of your own.

ADDITIONAL WORK ON SUPPORT: ANALYZING INFORMATION AND ESSAYS

Exercise 5   *Analyzing Information*

Sometimes you collect information on a topic and then find the evidence is complicated or conflicting. If this happens, it can then be difficult to decide on a main point and to select appropriate support for that main point.

The following list has conflicting information about the future of the bald eagle:

1. The North American continent had approximately 100,000 bald eagles in the late 1700s.

2. In the 1960s, scientists estimated the bald eagle population at 500 pairs. The California population fell to 20 nesting pairs.

3. The bald eagle has been listed as an "endangered species," a species facing possible extinction.

4. DDT, a pesticide, was introduced in 1940 and widely used in the United States during the 1950s and 1960s.

5. DDT accumulates in the fatty tissues of birds, fish, and mammals. Because the main diet of the eagle is fish and carrion (flesh from dead birds and animals), DDT reaches high concentrations in this predator.

6. DDT appears to affect eagle reproduction in several ways, including delaying the sexual maturity of the birds and causing them to lay thin-shelled eggs, which break before the eaglet is ready to hatch.

7. In 1972, DDT was banned. Other pesticides have replaced it.

8. At the Patuxent Wildlife Research Center, the U.S. Fish and Wildlife Service hatches eaglets and places them in the wild with eagle "foster parents" who have no young of their own.

9. The government once proposed ending the Patuxent Program, but Congress overruled the proposal.

10. The Patuxent Program has returned 44 bald eagles to the wild.

11. There is a flourishing black market in eagle feathers.

12. In one recent year, an estimated 250 eagles were killed by people either accidentally or deliberately.

13. The budget for the U.S. Fish and Wildlife Service—the agency that protects endangered species—has been cut substantially.

14. Currently, about 1,200 bald eagle pairs are known to exist in the United States (excluding Alaska).

15. In 1986, the bald eagle population in Alaska was estimated at 7,500 pairs.

16. The San Francisco Zoological Society has started a captive breeding program. The society hopes by 1991 to be producing 24 eaglets a year for release into the wild.

17. Birds raised in captivity have a difficult time adjusting to the wild and must be provided food for several months before they learn to hunt on their own.

Some experts predict that the eagle will survive; others think this bird will be extinct before the year 2000. Construct a main point giving your prediction about the future of the bald eagle:

_____

_____

Which of the items above would you use in supporting your prediction? #_____ #_____ #_____ #_____ #_____ #_____

Exercise 6   *Analyzing Information*

Sometimes in working with a broad topic you accumulate information that could support many different general ideas about the topic. You must sift through the material, searching for an idea you wish to explore further.

The material in the following list has some facts and details about television as well as general ideas about this broad topic. You couldn't use everything in the list in any one piece of writing.

In looking over the list of "possible meanings," several ideas seem to emerge: that the watch is cheap, that it is simple and functional, and that it has seen better days. If you were writing a short description of the watch, any one of these ideas might serve as a main point.

Group Activity 1   *Analyzing an Object*

As a group, select a simple object that is close at hand, such as a textbook, a pocketknife, a bookbag, or a jacket. Examine the object, having one member of the group list whatever details the group observes. Then go over the list and consider the possible meaning of each of the details. List these to the right of the details. When you have finished, read over the possible meanings, looking for a pattern of ideas or an overall conclusion they may suggest about the object. Record these beneath the list.

OBJECT:

Details   *Possible Meanings*

Overall ideas or conclusion:

Group Activity 2   *Analyzing a Photograph*

Examine the photograph below.

"Migrant Mother," Dorothea Lange, 1936.

Make a list of all the details you notice. Who is in the photograph? What are they doing? What terms would you use to describe the woman's clothing? How is she holding the child?

After you have put down every detail you notice, go over your list. To the right of each detail, write down what you think that detail implies about the possible meaning of the photograph. For example, what does the way the woman brings her hand to her mouth suggest about her feelings?

When you have finished listing the possible meanings of details, read through the list and consider what it suggests about the overall meaning of the photograph. Try to suggest at least two conclusions as to the meaning of the scene.

"MIGRANT MOTHER"

Details	*Possible Meaning*

Possible overall meanings:

1.

2.

Example: Analyzing an Event

The double-listing technique for analyzing in depth can also be applied to more complex topics. The following example shows how it may be used to analyze an *event:*

EVENT: A WEDDING

Details	*Possible Meanings*
Bride's family very religious; no one in groom's family has been to church in the last twenty years.	Serious differences right from the start?
Orange bridesmaids' gowns and brown tuxes for ushers.	Clunky colors—not the right spirit for a spring wedding.
Groom looked pale and shaky.	Hung over from bachelor party or maybe just nervous.
Bride's father gave her a look of pride and love as he walked her down the aisle.	???

Bride's mother cried during ceremony.	Probably doesn't mean anything—this happens at a lot of weddings.
Photographer was everywhere during ceremony; delayed reception 45 minutes taking more pictures.	Pictures seemed more important than the ceremony; delay seemed inconsiderate.
Reception line took forever.	Also inconsiderate; made the occasion seem like a duty rather than a celebration.
No alcohol served at the reception (held in the church social hall). This displeased some people.	The day didn't have a festive feeling.
A minor tussle during cake cutting; bride got a chinful of frosting and was furious.	A spirit of competition rather than cooperation; anger rather than fun.

Possible overall meaning:
The wedding was depressing, and the marriage seemed to get off to an unlucky start.

Writing Activity 1   *Analyzing an Event*

Choose an event that *you* recently witnessed or took part in.

1. On the left side of a piece of paper, list *all* the details you can recall about the event.
2. After you complete the list, read over it. To the right of each detail, list what you think the detail means or suggests about the event.
3. Write one or two sentences explaining what you think the event meant as a whole.

Writing Activity 2   *Analyzing the Teaching Habits of an Instructor*

1. On the left side of a piece of paper, list every detail you can about the teaching habits of one of your current or former instructors.
2. After you complete the list, review it and jot down to the right of each detail what you think that detail implies or suggests about the instructor's attitude toward teaching, toward the subject, or toward students.
3. Based on your analysis of this list, wirte one or two sentences summing up the instructor's teaching habits.

Writing Activity 3   *Analyzing Television Viewing Habits*

1. Analyze your own television viewing habits or those of someone you know well. Begin by listing every detail you can recall about these habits. (What kinds of shows are watched? When? How much television is watched each day? What else takes place during television viewing?)

2. After you complete the list, review it and write down what you think each detail suggests about the meaning or significance of the viewing habits. (Is the television viewing valuable or a waste of time? Is it interfering with relationships or other activities?)

3. Based on your analysis of this list, write one or two sentences describing the overall significance of the television viewing habits.

DECENTERING

Humans have a tendency to see the world from the perspective of their immediate personal experience. This tendency to be *self-centered* is natural and necessary, but it can also be limiting. A person's ability to think and to write is strengthened by moving out from the center of the self to a larger world of ideas and information. This *decentering* process may be thought of in terms of a circle that widens when you consider information from sources outside yourself:

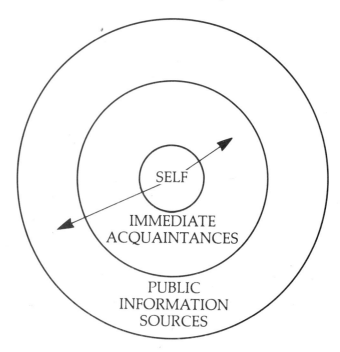

Decentering lets you bring a wider perspective and more information to any topic you write about. Of course, in moving outside your own experience, you should not simply accept new ideas without challenge. As you explore, make sense of, and write about the events that touch and form your world, you do so by squaring these events with your past experience. In the process of decentering, some of your views may change as you encounter new information, but *you* are still at the center of your thinking and of any writing you may do on a topic.

The following examples show the development of a paper written on the topic "Changes in Family Life." In exploring her topic the writer goes through a three-stage decentering process:

Stage One: Getting Ideas from the Self

The writer begins her writing process with a cluster that explores her own family background; she then does some discovery writing that "sums up" this cluster.

Stage Two: Getting Ideas from Immediate Acquaintances

The writer next starts to decenter her viewpoint by discussing the topic with friends and acquaintances, recording any new information in several brainstorming lists and in another cluster.

Stage Three: Getting Ideas from Public Sources of Information

Becoming interested in two different ideas, the writer explores each of them through further decentering in which she consults several public sources of information.

The rough plan and the paper that result from this decentering make use of information and ideas that the writer developed at each stage of the decentering process.

Decentering Examples: Stage One (Self)

The writer begins with a cluster, reproduced on the following page, on "changes in my own family."

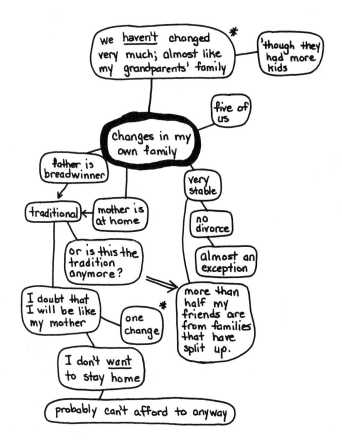

On the basis of the cluster, the writer tries to sum up her ideas in a discovery writing:

Changes in Family Life

My family is so normal, it's almost abnormal. When I look at people I know, I can see plenty of changes and problems in family life: divorce, both parents working, stepparents, single parents, fathers who do some of the things that the woman of the house used to do (shopping, raising children), etc. And when I look outside our family, it seems that the family is not such a strong unit as it once was. But it's hard for me to say much about this because my own family is pretty strong. We have our problems, of course—all families do—but our family hasn't changed that much. My parents have never been divorced, and my mom has always stayed home to look after the children. In most ways, we are a very traditional family. I can see myself changing, however. I want to have a career as well as a family, and so the family that I raise will have to be different from the family that I grew up in. That's one thing I could write about—how women in a family now have to do even more than before. But divorce is another possible topic, since many of the changes in family life begin when the parents split up. In a way, divorce seems like the biggest single change in family life today.

Decentering Examples: Stage Two (Immediate Acquaintances)

Once the writer has a sense of where she stands with regard to the topic, she can begin to decenter by discussing the topic with people she knows. Through such discussion, she will not only learn more about her topic, but will also begin to develop a feel for how her audience, her readers, may respond to her writing. The writer of this paper interviewed a neighbor, a librarian, her sister-in-law, and her nephew and niece. She recorded the information in a form similar to brainstorming lists, and then tried to sum up what she had learned in a discovery writing.

Cheryl (neighbor; single mother)

Has been divorced for four years; ex-husband has remarried. Works part time as copy editor for newspaper.

Feels that being a single mother and a worker is a stress, but enjoys each role.

Thinks that divorce changes the family ("obviously") but "doesn't destroy it."

Her two children live with her but go to father's place every other weekend.

She thinks it is important for children to have someone as a father figure.

Thinks it is possible for sense of family to survive even after husband and wife split up.

Family changes from tight structure to looser one.

Children have two ("or one and a half") families now.

Cheryl and her children spend a lot of time with her brother and his family—cousins are like brothers and sisters.

Feels that it is important that changes between parents not be made into changes between parents and children.

Ex-partners must learn not to bring children into arguments; this can be tough to avoid.

Thinks that in some cases children may be better off after a divorce if the relationship between husband and wife was hateful.

But also thinks that divorce is bound to hurt children in some sense.

Overall, sees divorce as fact of life and big change in family life; doesn't see any easy answers in the situation of more children living in divorced families.

<u>Children's librarian (working mother; not divorced)</u>

Enjoys her job and having many different roles: librarian, mother, wife.

As a librarian sees that there is a problem with latch-key children—children whose parents work and who have to take care of themselves after school.

Several latch-key children come to the library each day after school, wait there until parents come to pick them up.

> Bored, restless—have been sitting in class most of the day.

> No food, snacks.

> No way to work out energy; sometimes get into trouble.

> Can disrupt library.

Thinks a real day-care program would be better for these children.

> Provide after-school snack.

> Give chance for supervised play.

> More activities and someone to talk to.
(This would help library be a library, too.)

Says some parents don't arrive until after library closes; children sometimes have to wait outside in the dark; police may be called.

Parents are not poor and seem to care for their kids, but are <u>very busy</u>.

<u>Marjorie (sister-in-law; works in day-care center)</u>

Has to work to make ends meet; says that being a mother and a wife and a worker can be a strain, but necessary.

> Points out that Bob (husband) also has to do more now; they share chores around the condo, shopping, etc.

> Thinks being a parent and a worker may be a little harder for women.

Likes working with children in center but does not see it as career.

Thinks children at her center receive good care, perhaps better than other places.

Thinks many kids benefit from being around lots of other children.

> Learn social skills.

> Learn language skills, physical skills.

Thinks day-care centers are necessary but also wonders about effect on some children with very busy parents: a few parents just "dump their kids off at the curb."

Says there is a huge demand.

> Waiting list is three months.

<u>Ginny and Kurt (niece and nephew; ages 4 and 5)</u>

They think preschool is great.

Like playing with other children; each is in a different gang.

<u>Love</u> Mrs. Mays (director of school).

Liked the Thanksgiving party (G. was Indian; K. was pilgrim.).

Like drawing and painting.

Kurt likes to read.

Kurt is looking forward to going to kindergarten next semester. Ginny says so too, but she'll have to wait.

Note: Preschool has helped them get ready for school. They're better now at paying attention and sharing things, and they get along better with other children. It's also helped to make Ginny less dependent on Kurt—they're in different classes.

In a discovery writing, the writer attempts to put together some of the ideas she came across in speaking with other people:

In talking with other people about the ways that family life is changing, I've come across two main ideas. There's still the problem of divorce, how that's changing the family. But as Cheryl pointed out, there aren't any easy answers to how divorce changes family life. It changes families in so many different ways—making the family something that's split up, making the family wider in a way, and yet also smaller, bringing more people into the family relationship. (More people, but maybe the ties aren't as strong.) So perhaps I could write about how divorce changes family life.

But I'm also interested in another idea. Marjorie and Mrs. Woolf (the librarian) told me something about how family life is changing for working mothers, but they also brought up another topic—how children are being cared for differently nowadays. I was raised almost completely within my family, but today many children are raised by other people in addition to their parents. This change comes about because of more divorces but also because today both parents often have to work. In some ways this change seems bad (the latch-key children hanging around the library), but in other ways it may be a good thing: Ginny and Kurt love going to preschool, and I think it helps them develop so they'll do better in school. And it's probably necessary—how can a single parent get by, hold a job, without someone to watch the kids?

Decentering Examples: Stage Three (Public Sources of Information)

To find out more about the two topics (divorce and changes in child care) that most interest her, the writer consults a variety of public information sources: newspapers, magazines, books, and radio and television programs. She records the information from these sources in a manner similar to brainstorming lists.

Newspaper Article on Divorce

(Aurora Mackey, "Children Sketch Trauma on Divorce," L.A. Times, 23 Feb. 1987, part v: 1+)

Talks about drawings collected by family counselor (Florence Bienenfeld). The drawings were made by children waiting outside her office, "Where their parents frequently battled over child custody and visitation issues." (p. 1)

Pictures show "anger, frustration, loneliness, and fear." (p. 1)

Bienenfeld feels children and parents go through stages of recovery after a divorce.

> First stage is disbelief: some children draw pictures of parents still together.

Children are likely to be more disturbed if they don't have contact with both parents.

Children can be hurt if forced to take sides against one parent. (Cheryl mentions this too.)

In 1986 L.A. County had "42,000 filing for dissolution." (p. 2)

> 60% of these involve children under 18

Bienenfeld makes a good point: "The family is a system. Children are incredibly resilient and you can help them through their feelings about the divorce." (p. 2)

Article on Children and Welfare

("Sounder of Alarms," Time Magazine, Feb. 16, 1987, p. 21)

"The stable two-parent family is becoming the exception rather than the norm, and 12 million children are growing up in poverty and with inadequate training for the job market."

Article on Child Care

(Karen Rubin, "Whose Job Is Child Care?" Ms. Magazine, March 1987, pp. 32-44.)

One reason there aren't more child-care programs is the idea that the father is the sole breadwinner in most families. (p. 42)

> Actually, only 10% of American families have father as sole breadwinner. (p. 42)

"Our society has to help make it possible for people to have families— either corporations must take some responsibility, or there has to be government-paid maternity leave for a reasonable length of time, quality subsidized child care, and job security." (p. 42—Karen Nussbaum, executive director of 9 to 5, National Association of Working Women)

Some large companies (IBM, Campbell Soup) sponsor child-care programs for their employees. (p. 40)

"In Europe good, inexpensive child care is available to everybody. All kinds of changes will be needed when we recognize that care of little children is the most important work being done and the responsibility of the whole society." (p. 44—Caroline Bird, writer)

Radio News Program on Child Care

(Can't remember date; program presented on National Public Radio)

Program discussed a child-care project for handicapped children.

Parents of severely handicapped children have a very hard time finding anyone to provide temporary care (a few days to week or two) for their children.

This can cause real problems in a marriage—partners never get a chance to have time to themselves.

Program allows parents to go on a short trip or vacation, which otherwise would be impossible.

There are only a few programs like this in the U.S.

Book on Day Care

(Margaret O'Brien Steinfels, Who's Minding the Children? [New York: Simon & Schuster, 1973])

Author's main point seems to be that day care shouldn't be seen as a threat to family life:

"Day care should confirm the importance of child-rearing and the parents' role in it; day care should not be defined as a substitute for family but as a support and supplement for it." (p. 242)

Day care should support the bond between parents and children, not come between them. (p. 238)

Day care is not a simple topic; there isn't any one right form of day care.

"Different families need different kinds of day care." (p. 237)

Author thinks it's important for parents to be actively involved in any day-care program they send their children to.

Newspaper Article on Law and Families

(Roxane Arnold, "Fatherhood: Law Facing a Challenge," L.A. Times, 5 Mar. 1987, part ii: 1+)

"I think modern society has essentially redefined our notion of the family unit. To rely on a traditional notion ignores the social reality." (Michael L. Oddenino, National Council for Children's Rights, Inc.)

Example: Shaping and Arranging Ideas

Having gone through the decentering process, the writer had a much better idea of what she wanted to write about. She decided to write on the topic "changes in the way children are cared for," using as a possible main point the following idea:

Social conditions have changed, so we must change the way we raise children.

Focusing on this idea, the writer went back through her decentering materials and made a cluster, pulling in ideas she wanted to use in her paper.

Notice that the writer was able to use material from each stage of the decentering process and that she was able to apply information from the topic of divorce to the topic she chose to write about: changes in the way children are cared for.

Example: Making a Rough Plan

Having identified in the cluster the ideas she wants to bring into her paper, the writer next constructs a rough plan that puts these ideas in a logical order:

Rough Plan

<u>Main point:</u> Social conditions have changed, so we must change the way we raise children.

> Changes in society affect family.
> > Society is busier, more complex.
> > Family not as stable.
> > > Working parents.
> > > Divorce.

> Traditional ways of caring for children no longer work as well as they once did.

> We need to try new ways of caring for children.
> > More day care.
> > Better day care.
> > New idea of family.

Example: Paper Written After Decentering

The writer uses the rough plan as a guide for her paper, but does not follow it exactly. In the paper, the writer draws on material developed in each stage of her decentering process.

Changes in Family Life: Caring for Children

I grew up in a very traditional family. My father was the breadwinner, and my mother ran the house and looked after the children. The family structure that I knew as a child was very similar to the family structure that my parents knew when they were young. Today this kind of family structure is becoming almost abnormal. Society is changing, and this changes what families are like. One of the parts of family life that is changing the fastest is the way children are cared for. I believe that changes in family life make it important to find new and better ways to raise children.

Society is constantly growing more complex and getting busier and busier. As a result, the family unit is becoming much less stable. Nowadays, both parents may have to work to provide enough money to buy food and shelter for the family. Because both parents are working, there is less time for the kind of close personal relations that hold a family together. This causes even families with two parents to become less stable.

But today many families have only a single parent at home, and this makes family life even less stable. The divorce rate is very high, especially here in Los Angeles. For example, one writer has pointed out that there were more than 42,000 divorces in L.A. County (Mackey, p. 1). This means that thousands of single parents, most of them women, have to take on three jobs at once: earning money, looking after the home, and raising children. It's almost impossible for one person to do all three of these jobs well.

Because the family structure is less stable today, traditional ways of caring for children no longer work as well as they once did. In my "traditional" family, one parent—my mother—had responsibility for taking care of the children when they came home from school. Today, however, many children come home to an empty house. These latch-key children must learn to take care of themselves at home or find someplace such as a library where they can wait for their parents. As another example, my father used to serve as the enforcer in our family—if one of us children did something especially bad, Dad would provide stern discipline. Many of my friends no longer have fathers who live at home, and because of this some of them get away with very wild behavior or get into fights with their mothers, who have to provide all the discipline themselves.

If traditional methods of caring for children no longer work, then we should consider new methods. Day care is one such method. At the present time, the demand for day care is much greater than can be met. Some large companies, such as IBM and Campbell Soup, provide day care programs for their workers, but most parents have a difficult time finding quality care for their children. My sister-in-law told me that there is a three-month waiting list at the day-care center where she works. It's obvious, looking at the needs of working parents and the demand for day care, that something should be done to open more centers.

Along with getting more day-care centers, I think we also need to change the attitude society has about day care. A day-care center does not have to be seen as a place where children are dumped while their parents work. Day care doesn't have to be seen as a danger to family life. Instead, day care can be seen as a way to help children grow up right at a time when social changes make that harder and harder to do. As Margaret O'Brien Steinfels has said, "Day care should not be defined as a substitute for family but as a support and supplement for it" (p. 242).

Family life is changing more quickly than ever before, and there is a great need to find ways to care for the children that are caught up in these changes. Day-care programs, if used wisely, can help to give children some of the stability they may lose as family life changes.

Sources

Aurora Mackey, "Children Sketch Trauma on Divorce," L.A. Times. 23 Feb. 1987, part v: 1+.

Margaret O'Brien Steinfels, Who's Minding the Children? (New York: Simon & Schuster, 1973).

Group Activity 3   *Decentering*

Select a topic that the whole group would like to explore, or use one provided by your instructor. Then, as a group, do a cluster or brainstorming list to get down your first ideas about the topic.

Next, make a list of your immediate acquaintances who might be consulted to find out more about the topic. Each person in the group should try to contribute one or two names to this list.

Finally, make a list of the sources of public information that might be used to inquire further into the topic. Consider newspapers, magazines, specific books or types of books, and radio and TV programs that relate to the topic. Again, each member of the group should contribute one or two suggestions.

Topic:

List of immediate acquaintances to consult:

List of public sources of information to consult:

Writing Activity 4   *Decentering (Stage One: Self)*

Select a writing topic that you are interested in, or use one suggested by your instructor. Consider an issue you have already touched on in your Writer's Notebook, or an issue such as one of the following:

Science and society
Military spending
Religion, politics, and education
American technology

Begin the decentering process by doing a cluster or brainstorming list to record your initial thoughts about the topic you have selected. (See the example on pp. 105–106.)

Next, read over your cluster or brainstorming list and then do a short discovery writing to sum up your ideas about the topic and to consider possible directions you might want to follow as you continue to decenter. (See the example on pp. 106–107.)

Writing Activity 5   *Decentering (Stage Two: Immediate Acquaintances)*

Think of three or four of your immediate acquaintances who might have ideas concerning the topic you selected in Writing Activity 4. These people do not need to be experts on the topic but merely people who have had some experience related to it.

Once you have several persons in mind, read over your discovery writing for the Writing Activity, looking for questions or issues to discuss with them. On a separate piece of paper, make note of any questions or discussion points that occur to you.

Arrange a brief period when you can interview each of the acquaintances you have selected. When you interview the person, use your list of discussion points and questions to guide the discussion, but remain open to any new issues or directions that come up during the interview. (For instance, in the example on pp. 107–108, the discussion began on the issue of working mothers but then shifted to the problem of latch-key children.)

Record the responses of the person as carefully as possible. If you think you might later wish to quote anything the person says, use quotation marks (" ") to indicate exactly what was said. (See the example on pp. 107–108.)

After you interview at least two or three people who might be able to help you decenter your thinking, go over your notes to the interviews and do a short discovery writing to sum up your new position on the topic. (See the example on p. 109.)

Writing Activity 6   *Decentering (Stage Three: Public Sources of Information)*

Read over the discovery writing you completed for Writing Activity 5 and decide on one or two areas within the original topic that you would like to explore further. Then look for public sources of information to provide further ideas about these areas. Consider using:

Newspaper articles

Magazine articles

Books

Radio or TV programs

Find at least three sources and take careful notes on each. (See the examples on pp. 109–111.) When you have finished, go over all the information you have collected during your decentering process and decide on a possible main point. (See the example on p. 111.)

Chapter 8
*Revising the Whole Paper*___

- Looking at Your Own Revision Process
- Reading for Revision
  - First Impressions
  - Description
  - Evaluation
- Using Evaluations to Make a Revision Plan
- Additional Help with Revision
  - Checking Your Paragraphs
  - Checking Your Introduction
  - Checking Your Conclusion
  - Checking Your Transitions
  - Checking Your Sentence Structure and Mechanics
- Format of a Paper

LOOKING AT YOUR OWN REVISION PROCESS___

Many writers believe they have to get everything right the first time. They're wrong. *Revision* is a process that goes on continuously in the writer's head and on paper. You revise all the time—even when you're not aware of it.

You already know a great deal about revision, of course. In the preceding chapters, you have learned how to make changes as you work through a paper:

- [ ] To find a focus in a jumble of material
- [ ] To move from lack of organization to clear patterns of order
- [ ] To adjust your main point
- [ ] To explore a topic again if more support is needed
- [ ] To inquire further if your analysis is not adequate or you need more information

You have been using these revision techniques to make changes in your own writing. In this chapter, you will study the revision process itself in order to develop and practice your own revision methods. The revision process consists of two general stages:

Looking closely at what you have written in order to see what changes you want to make

Making those changes

Revision can involve rewriting a whole paper or tinkering with a small part of it. In either case, you decide what changes you want to make and then make them.

The revision process is different for every writer. Some complete a whole draft before reworking it; others stop every few sentences to reread and revise. Complete the Writing Activity below to discover your methods of revision.

Writing Activity 1   *Writer's Inventory*

In your Writer's Notebook, respond to the following questions. Then complete the Group Activity that follows.

Writer's Inventory: Revision

1. How many drafts do you usually write for one paper?

2. How much do you write before you read over what you've written? A sentence? A paragraph? The whole paper?

3. Do you change things in your writing as you go along, or do you write an entire draft without stopping?

4. Do you show drafts of papers to anyone?

5. What is your usual reaction to early drafts of your papers?

6. When you finish a draft, do you ever put it away for a while before you read it?

7. Have you ever thrown away an entire draft of a paper and started over again?

8. What changes have you already made in your writing habits? What changes might you make in the future?

Group Activity 1   *Recognizing Your Revising Habits*

In a small group, share your responses to each of the questions above. Discuss the following questions:

1. What do your answers to these writer's inventory questions tell you about the way you revise?

2. How do your methods differ from those of others in the group?

3. Listening to others in the group, can you recognize your own revising habits?

READING FOR REVISION

Reading over what you have written is a key skill in revising a paper. Some people write a few sentences before they reread and revise them. Others write longer passages before rereading and revising. As you discover your own style of revision, you will sense how much to write before you read over and rewrite. The point here is that to revise you must first read critically; you must become your own audience.

You can help train yourself to read your own papers more thoroughly and critically by actually assuming the role of reader and reading other people's writing. Below we have outlined a reading technique that will help you read another person's papers and then your own. This process can be divided into three steps:

1. First impressions
2. Description
3. Evaluation

Suggestions for Readers

Whenever you give feedback on some else's paper:

- [ ] **Always read through the <u>whole</u> paper before discussing any of its parts.**
- [ ] **Find out from the paper what the writer is trying to say; don't impose your own ideas on the paper.**
- [ ] **Be honest, but stress the positive; start with what is best about a paper.**

First Impressions

In revision you need to reread and rethink what you have written before changing it. The easiest way to do this is to read a piece of writing quickly to get your first or "gut" reaction to it. This first reading looks at the overall purpose and performance of a piece of writing without paying too much attention to specific features or isolating individual problems.

In this first reading of a paper, you might ask a series of questions:

1. Do I like this paper? Why or why not?
2. What's it about?
3. Is it interesting?
4. What are its strengths and weaknesses?
5. What else do I want to know about the topic?
6. Overall, what is my impression of this paper?

Writing Activity 2   *First Impressions*

Read the paper on vandalism on page 122 and then write your first impressions of it in a short paragraph, using the questions listed below to guide you. Keep your analysis; you may use it again shortly.

1. Do I like this paper? Why or why not?
2. What's it about?
3. Is it interesting?
4. What are its strengths or weaknesses?
5. What else do I want to know about the topic?
6. Overall, what is my impression of this paper?

Description

Before you can revise a paper, you must decide what needs to be changed. The quick reading is an important step in the revision process, but your first impressions may or may not hold up under closer analysis. The best way to know what is in a piece of writing is to *describe* it and *evaluate* it.

A *description* is a detailed account of the content and structure of a piece of writing. In writing a description, go through the paper and decide what the writer has done in each section or paragraph. Ask yourself these questions:

What is the writer trying to convince me of or show me?

What point is the writer making?

Avoid too much quotation from the paper; use your own words instead. Be sure to describe the paper without saying what is right or wrong with it. A description describes; it does not make evaluations.

A description of the vandalism paper is on page 123.

Evaluation

After you have described a piece of writing, you know *what* has been said. You are now much better prepared to evaluate this piece of writing point by point. In an evaluation you comment on what works or doesn't work in the paper, question the writer if you are confused about anything, and make suggestions about possible revisions. A description tells what is in a paper. An evaluation tells what you think of it and how it might be changed.

In evaluating any piece of writing:

1. Write a point-by-point evaluation of the paper as you did above in the description. It may be easiest, as above, to write your evaluation on a sheet of paper placed next to the original paper.

2. Ask these questions as you go through the paper:
   a. Is this paper held together by a clear main point?
   b. Does the writer provide enough support and detail for this point?
   c. Are the ideas in the paper clearly organized?
   d. Is the sentence structure complete? Is the language clear?
   e. Is the paper interesting?
   f. Does the paper have a good introduction and conclusion?

3. When you don't understand a point or any section of the paper, write down questions.

4. Make concrete suggestions for ways you think the writer might improve the paper.

5. Conclude with a summary evaluation of the paper.

On p. 125 is a point-by-point evaluation of the vandalism paper. Notice that the evaluation includes comments, questions, suggestions for revision, and a summary evaluation.

The summary at the end of the evaluation provides a short analysis of the major strengths and weaknesses of the paper and makes specific suggestions for revision. It may be the most valuable response a writer can get. A summary evaluation looks like the first-impressions reading of a paper that you did at the beginning of this chapter, and it may confirm some of the things you noticed in that first, quick reading, but a summary evaluation is based on a closer analysis of the paper and therefore provides a stronger set of recommendations for revision.

With the three reading techniques—recording first impressions, describing, and evaluating—you are learning close reading of other people's writing and, finally, of your own. Before you can effectively revise your own writing, you have to be able to *read* what you have written to see what is in it and to know how it can be changed.

Vandalism: A Serious Campus Problem

We can hardly walk across campus lately without being reminded of campus vandalism. We read about it in the newspaper and see signs posted about it. We're also reminded of campus vandalism by the actual damage we see.

The type of vandalism that is getting a lot of attention on campus right now is the destruction of property. Most of this destruction is the result of carelessness and selfishness. People litter public areas and let off steam by turning over campus park benches. All of this destruction is irritating and expensive.

Another type of vandalism that seems serious to me is that which is aimed at groups of people and individuals. Recently, signs put up by a campus anti-apartheid group were torn down. Graffiti on restroom walls make terrible comments about people. Several weeks ago, a girl who isn't very popular at school was the victim of vandalism. She has always been made fun of by a certain group of students, but this time, they got into her dorm room. They dumped things out of drawers and off of shelves, wrote cruel remarks on her mirror, and made a general mess of her room. A faculty member's car was vandalized because he spoke out in favor of eliminating football at the school.

All of these acts of vandalism are a campus problem. To destroy campus property costs the school money. But at least property can be replaced. The most serious type of vandalism is that which attempts to destroy the reputation of a group or of a particular person. It is especially serious when acts of vandalism are directed toward individuals who cannot protect themselves.

I hope that you will think about what you are doing the next time you litter the lawn, write on walls, or destroy property in some way. Why are you doing it? We all need to be concerned.

Example Description of Vandalism Paper

Paragraph 1: The writer is making the point that vandalism is a serious problem on campus. We see it everywhere.

Paragraph 2: One type of vandalism is the destruction of property, which results from carelessness or selfishness. The writer gives examples of this type and makes the point that it's irritating and expensive.

Paragraph 3: The writer describes another type of vandalism, that is aimed at groups or individuals. The writer gives examples of vandalism against both groups and individuals.

Paragraph 4: Here the writer makes the point that although both of these types of vandalism are serious, the most serious is the type aimed at groups of people and individuals. The writer ends by saying the worst type is that aimed at individuals who can't protect themselves.

Paragraph 5: The writer concludes the paper by asking the reader to think carefully before vandalizing.

Vandalism: A Serious Campus Problem

We can hardly walk across campus lately without being reminded of campus vandalism. We read about it in the newspaper and see signs posted about it. We're also reminded of campus vandalism by the actual damage we see.

The type of vandalism that is getting a lot of attention on campus right now is the destruction of property. Most of this destruction is the result of carelessness and selfishness. People litter public areas and let off steam by turning over campus park benches. All of this destruction is irritating and expensive.

Another type of vandalism that seems serious to me is that which is aimed at groups of people and individuals. Recently, signs put up by a campus anti-apartheid group were torn down. Graffiti on restroom walls make terrible comments about people. Several weeks ago, a girl who isn't very popular at school was the victim of vandalism. She has always been made fun of by a certain group of students, but this time, they got into her dorm room. They dumped things out of drawers and off of shelves, wrote cruel remarks on her mirror, and made a general mess of her room. A faculty member's car was vandalized because he spoke out in favor of eliminating football at the school.

All of these acts of vandalism are a campus problem. To destroy campus property costs the school money. But at least property can be replaced. The most serious type of vandalism is that which attempts to destroy the reputation of a group or of a particular person. It is especially serious when acts of vandalism are directed toward individuals who cannot protect themselves.

I hope that you will think about what you are doing the next time you litter the lawn, write on walls, or destroy property in some way. Why are you doing it? We all need to be concerned.

Notes for Evaluation

<u>Paragraph 1</u>: The introduction states the topic clearly. The reader might feel more involved if the writer told more about the specific reminders. What newspaper? What kind of signs? Also, in the last paragraph the writer makes an important point about which kind of vandalism is the most serious. I think that's the most important part of the paper. Shouldn't it go in the introduction?

<u>Paragraph 2</u>: I would get more involved and initated myself if the writer showed more vandalism.

<u>Paragraph 3</u>: I started to get interested here. Paragraph 3 really made me think about vandalism in a new way, especially after I read the last paragraph. What makes people aim vandalism at groups? Paragraph 3 begins to bring out the difference between vandalism toward individuals and toward groups. The writer might want to say more about the two types. What kind of comments are made on bathroom walls?

<u>Paragraph 4</u>: Again, I'd like to know more about the two more personal types of vandalism. Why is vandalism directed against individuals more serious? Interesting idea.

<u>Paragraph 5</u>: I felt strange reading this because I don't vandalize. What does the writer want me to do?

<u>Summary</u>: There are some very strong ideas and support in this paper, but I think the main point needs to be strengthened. The point really is that vandalism against individuals is the most serious. Organization is OK except in last paragraph. I don't know what it does for the paper. Also, paragraph 3 could really be two paragraphs. Support — The writer needs more examples and detail all through the paper. (See notes in evaluation above.) I think this paper makes a valuable point. I'd never thought about vandalism in this way before. The paper made me think. It's worth a revision.

USING EVALUATION TO MAKE A REVISION PLAN_____

You do a close reading of a paper for one purpose: to discover what needs to be changed. After you have read it closely, you are ready to revise it.

But what do you do with an evaluation of your writing? How do you move from evaluation to revision?

☐   First, think about the suggestions that you and other readers have made on a particular piece of writing.

☐   Next, decide what changes, if any, you want to make.

☐   Finally, make those changes in the paper itself.

The first thing to do in revision, then, is to reread your own paper with the evaluations in mind to decide what should be changed. Often you need to translate the evaluator's comments (your own, a teacher's, or a fellow student's) into terms of revision.

The Revision Guide on p. 135 takes comments you might typically find in an evaluation of a paper and transfers them into revision guidelines.

The author of "Vandalism: A Serious Campus Problem" went over his paper and the evaluations. Then he wrote the following:

Notes for Revision

1. Problems with main point: Make main point clearer. Pick up idea of acts of vandalism against groups and individuals and point out which is most serious.

2. Problems with organization: Paragraph 3 should be split into two paragraphs to show two types of vandalism against people. Consider eliminating last paragraph. Doesn't do much for paper.

3. Problems with support: All paragraphs need more specific detail, especially paragraphs 2 and 3. I need to show more acts of vandalism and show why acts against people are more serious.

4. Introduction and conclusion must convince people that there is a problem. I could use more detail.

5. Sentence structure and language: I need to read the paper out loud to catch rough spots. In adding detail, I'll pay attention to using specific language.

After writing the notes for revision above, the writer made the rough plan below.

Rough Plan

<u>Main point:</u> Although we see many types of vandalism on campus, the most destructive is the type that degrades people.

1. Things that remind us of vandalism on campus

    Newspaper
    Signs
    Actual vandalism

2. Acts of vandalism that people commit out of carelessness and to get attention

    Littering
    Walking on grass
    Food fights
    Destroying library books

3. Not worst types of vandalism

4. Acts of vandalism that are directed at groups of people

    Against anti-apartheid groups
    Graffiti on restroom walls
      racial slurs
      gays

5. Destructive acts aimed at individuals

    Girl's dorm room broken into
    Student's notes ripped up
    Faculty member's tires slashed

6. Worst type directed against individuals

    Property can be replaced.
    Groups can rely on support from members.
    Individuals are vulnerable because they are least able to protect themselves.

With these revision notes and a rough plan in front of him, the writer went over his paper and rewrote it. The revised draft appears on the next page.

Vandalism: A Serious Campus Problem

We can hardly walk across campus lately without being reminded of campus vandalism. The campus newspaper has been running stories and pictures covering the vandalism, and signs posted in most public areas remind us in red letters that damaging public property is against the law. We are also reminded of campus vandalism by the actual damage we see: broken windows, graffiti, litter. But I have come to realize that although we see many types of vandalism on campus, the most destructive type is not the vandalism that destroys property. The most destructive type is that which degrades people.

The type of vandalism that is getting the most attention on campus is the destruction of property. Most of this vandalism is the result of carelessness and selfishness. People walk across the grass and litter public areas without thinking. They let off steam by having food fights in the student lounge. Because they are too selfish or lazy, they cut pages out of library books rather than taking the time to copy what they need. All of this destruction is irritating and expensive, but it is not the most serious type of destruction.

The type of vandalism that seems the most serious to me is that which expresses hatred toward people and attempts to degrade them. Sometimes this vandalism is aimed at groups of people. Recently all the signs put up by the campus anti-apartheid group were pulled down. Graffiti on restroom walls frequently makes racial slurs or makes cruel remarks about gays.

Other destructive acts are aimed at individuals. For instance, several weeks ago, a girl who isn't very popular at school was the victim of vandalism. She has always been made fun of by a certain group of students, but this time, she was the victim of a cruel joke that got out of hand. They got into her dorm room and dumped things from shelves and drawers. They wrote cruel messages on her mirror in lipstick, and even put super-glue in the locks on her wardrobe doors. Another student, an accounting major who gets A's in all of his classes, had valuable notes destroyed while he was studying in the library. He walked away from the table where he had his books and notebook, and when he came back a few minutes later, someone had ripped up his notes. Another destructive act was aimed at a faculty member who spoke out in favor of dropping the school's football program because of recruiting scandals. His tires were slashed, and an obscene middle name was added to his office nameplate.

All of these acts of vandalism are a campus problem. To destroy campus property costs the school money. But at least property can be replaced. It is also serious when students attempt to destroy a group's reputation. But at least groups do have a certain strength in numbers. I feel that the most serious form of vandalism is the attempt to destroy the security or dignity of an individual. Individuals who are singled out in acts of vandalism are alone and vulnerable, and they are the least capable of protecting themselves.

ADITIONAL HELP WITH REVISION

It is often not until you begin reading for revision that you can get a feeling for the whole paper. In the revision stage you may recognize the importance of your paragraphs, introduction, conclusion, and transitions. In this section, we will give you a few guidelines for checking these parts of your papers.

Checking Your Paragraphs

A short paper may have only one paragraph. But in a longer paper that includes more ideas and information, additional paragraphs become necessary.

How do you recognize the need for a new paragraph? Often paragraphs develop as you write: when you come to a major new section of material, you need to start a new paragraph. Paragraphs should make it easier for readers to follow your ideas.

Look at the revised vandalism paper on page 128. Can you see the justification for each of its five paragraphs? Can you see the reason for the paragraph you are reading at this moment?

When you are reading a paper for revision, check to make sure that your paragraphs are helping you and your readers.

1. Are there too many ideas in any one paragraph? Does any paragraph need to be divided? Is any paragraph too long for a reader to get through comfortably?
2. Are any paragraphs too short? Can any of them be combined? Do you need more support and detail in any short paragraph?

Checking Your Introduction

1. *Purpose of an Introduction:* The first paragraph or two of your paper will serve as an introduction to the ideas you present in your paper. Through its content and tone, an introduction should accomplish the following:
   a. Interest your readers
   b. Persuade readers that what you have to say is valuable and worth reading
   c. Establish the purpose of your paper. Usually the introduction contains the point you are making. If the paper is quite long, you may even want to include a sentence or two giving the key ideas you will cover in the parts of your paper.

2. *Types of Introductions:* There is no one way to structure an introduction. As you craft the introductory paragraph or paragraphs of a paper, you might want to experiment with the different types of introductions described below. Diagrams have been provided to show possible ways to structure an introduction.

Type 1

Definition of Problem: Introduce your paper by giving your reader necessary background information on the issue you will discuss.

Overview or definition of the problem

Statement of the main point

In the example below, the problem is defined in the first part of the paragraph, and the statement of the main point follows.

Definition of the problem

> We can hardly walk across campus lately without being reminded of campus vandalism. The campus newspaper has been running stories and pictures covering the vandalism, and signs posted in most public areas remind us in red letters that damaging public property is against the law. We are also reminded of campus vandalism by the actual damage we see: broken windows, graffiti, litter. But I have come to realize that although we see many types of vandalism on campus, the most destructive type is not

Main point

> the vandalism that destroys property. The most destructive type is that which degrades people.

Type 2

Anecdote: In your introduction, relate an anecdote or brief story relevant to the issue you are discussing and end with a statement of the problem and your main point.

Relevant anecdote plus a statement of the problem

Statement of your main point

In the introduction below, the writer uses an anecdote to catch the reader's attention. Then the writer presents the main point.

Anecdote

> At supper recently, my wife and I were talking about how our five-year-old daughter, Coco, was getting to know more adults outside the family. Georgia asked Coco which adults she liked the most.
> "I only love Mommy," she answered with that magical but often painful twist of spontaneity.
> We waited for more of an answer. When nothing came, I tiptoed into the conversation. "You don't love Daddy?"

Anecdote

"I love you too Daddy but not as much as Mommy. I cry when Mommy goes away." (And from time to time, she does cry.) I shivered. I knew Coco was being honest. She was telling it like it is, with no harm intended.

Is this what I get for carefully doing my share of the child-care chores, I thought?

We fathers want the love. But are we willing to pay for it? Learning how to answer that question remains one of the hardest challenges I've ever faced.

Main point

For the past five years, I have gradually learned the skills necessary to help raise my own child, altering child-care schedules and adjusting my career all the while.

Bill Finger
The North Carolina Independent

Type 3

Questioning: In the introduction, take issue with a commonly held opinion or issue.

Statement of the opinion you don't agree with.

Statement of your main point.

In the example below, the author is taking issue with the commonly held opinion that the real danger of TV is the violence that is portrayed in most of the shows.

Opinion author questions

There have been a number of studies that have claimed to establish some statistical link between TV and violence. However, these studies establish at best that many poor, lonely, isolated and despairing individuals spend a lot of time looking at TV screens. The causes of the violence that occasionally explodes out of these people come more from already existing psychological, social or economic oppression than from the theatrical violence portrayed on TV.

Main point

However, TV causes a more serious and pervasive psychic violence in normal, less despairing youngsters who watch TV attentively and regularly. What results from this psychic abuse is the impoverishment of personality and the trivialization of life.

Herbert Kohl
"Physical Violence Aside,
TV's Psychic Violence Is the Real
Cause for Alarm"

Type 4

Quotation: Use a relevant quotation or aphorism or folk saying that introduces the idea you will make in your paper. You will probably want to follow the quotation with a sentence or two briefly explaining its relevance to your topic.

Quotation or aphorism or folk saying and its relevance to your topic

Statement of your main point

The following example uses a quotation to focus the reader's attention on the problem of boredom in our society.

Quotation

Recently, in an article by Sven Birkerts, the author commented on the widespread problem of boredom: "We have to face it: boredom is here, lodged in the culture, and it's spreading by the minute. It is the most splendid of ironies, really. For America is richer in options and entertainments than any society at any point in recorded history. We have access to every resource and vice. But go out and check for yourself. Walk through your city or town for just one day with your eyes open. . . . Wherever you turn, fingers are drumming, gazes are detached, and eyes are wandering," (Sven Birkerts, Boston Phoenix, July 22, 1986). I got to thinking about the problem, and I decided to do just that—to walk around with my eyes open for a week and look for evidence of boredom. I

Main point

was amazed. It seems that we really are a bored society. I see it in my classmates, my friends, my family, and my neighbors.

Sometimes it is best to wait until you have finished the first draft of your paper before you fine tune or even write your introduction. Sometimes you will find that you have difficulty getting started with your paper because you can't think of a good beginning strategy. If that happens, it is best to put your main point at the top of the page and let it guide you in developing your ideas. You can then go back and write an appropriate introductory paragraph when you revise your paper.

Checking Your Conclusion

The concluding paragraph should bring your paper to a graceful close. Conclusions can do several things.

1. *Interpret the ideas you have discussed in your paper.* This type of conclusion answers the question "So what?" or "What does all this information really add up to?"

2. *Summarize the main argument of your paper.* You may want to repeat your main point at the end of your paper. Rephrase that point, repeating key words.

3. *Suggest new directions.* A paper that has only a summary in its last paragraph takes its readers in a circle. You may want to give your readers something new to think about by suggesting possible solutions or new directions for your topic.

Checking Your Transitions

When revising, make sure that there are logical connections between parts of your paper. Transitions help your reader move smoothly from one section of your paper to another. Transitions are provided in a number of ways, but two of the most important are the repetition of key words and phrases and the use of transitional words and phrases.

1. The repetition of key words and phrases reminds your reader of your topic and your ideas about it. For instance, the repetition of the words "vandalism," "destroy," and "destruction" throughout the essay "Vandalism: A Serious Campus Problem" keeps the reader's attention focused on the problem of vandalism.

2. Transitional words and phrases function the same way as the repetition of key words and phrases. Below is a list of words that can help your readers see the connections between the ideas in your paper.

   a. To signal addition: *and, also, in addition, first, next, furthermore, besides, in the first place*

   b. To signal likeness: *similarly, likewise, equally important, again*

   c. To signal time: *next, afterward, at the same time, before, earlier, immediately, in the meantime, later, at last, when, then, finally, the following day*

   d. To signal contrast or disagreement: *but, on the contrary, in contrast, however, on the other hand, although, yet, nevertheless, meanwhile*

   e. to signal emphasis: *most important, most of all, especially, principally, chiefly*

   f. To signal illustration: *for example, for instance, in other words, specifically, because, as an illustration*

   g. To signal consequence or conclusion: *therefore, consequently, thus, as a result, in summary, in other words, in short, in conclusion, to sum up*

Checking Your Sentence Structure and Mechanics

While writing a discovery draft or other early version of a paper, you should not let worries about such things as sentence structure, spelling, and punctuation interrupt your writing process. But when you are preparing a piece of writing for a final, or public, draft, then you do need to look carefully at those areas. You may not be able to recognize and correct every problem with sentence structure and mechanics. However, Chapters 9 and 10 provide techniques to help you with this aspect of the revision process.

FORMAT OF A PAPER

When you have revised a paper and are ready to make a final draft, you need to pay attention to its format—the way the paper should look when you turn it in. Following are some guidelines for a paper's format.

The paper below has been typed so that it is clearer, but the points that are made apply to handwritten papers as well. Read the paper and the numbered rules at the same time. Use these rules for format whenever you write a paper.

1. Capitalize the first letters of first and main words in title. Don't use quotation marks.

2. Leave some space between the title and the body of the paper.

3. Indent the first paragraph (and every paragraph after that).

A Valuable Possession

My most valuable possession is my AM/FM radio-cassette player. It's the most expensive thing I own, and it's also a reminder that I have earned something all by myself.

I bought my radio with the money that I saved from working at a Burger King near my house. The radio cost $300, which is pretty high, but I felt I deserved a present for working at such a place for a full year.

My Sharpe GF3585 radio-cassette player in silver and black stands about a foot in height,

4. Maintain the margin on both sides of the paper.

is two inches wide, and weighs about twelve pounds. My radio is more than just a radio—it's a friend. Sometimes if I'm feeling a little down and out, I'll just turn on my radio and listen my worries or sadness away. If I'm bored, my radio allows me to pass the time away joyfully. I do my

5. Break words only between syllables.

homework completely and smoothly with a tape playing or with the radio on.

Every time I look at my radio, I smile *because* I'm looking at an accomplishment in my life. I earned that radio with my own sweat and aching muscles.

6. Leave space at bottom and top of the paper, and write or type only on one side of the page.

REVISION GUIDE

Comment from an Evaluation	Possible Problems	Possible Solutions
1. Paper is dull or uninteresting.	Your topic	Rethink the topic: Do I care about this topic? Do I know enough about it? (Chapter 3)
	Support	Explore your topic further to find more support. Add details. (Chapter 6)
2. Paper is confusing.	Your main point	Rethink your topic or narrow main point. (Chapters 3 and 4)
	Order, organization	Do an outline of your paper: Can any sections be cut? Rearranged? (Chapter 5)
3. Paper wanders, gets off the main idea.	Order, organization	Do an outline of your paper: Can any sections be cut? Rearranged? (Chapter 5)
4. You don't have enough evidence for your ideas.	Support, detail	Explore your topic further to find more support. Add details. (Chapter 6)
	Needs further inquiry	Analyze your topic in depth and/or broaden your perspective. (Chapter 7)
5. Ideas in the paper seem shallow.	Needs further inquiry	Analyze your topic in depth and/or broaden your perspective. (Chapter 7)
6. Good start, but needs more development.	Paper still an early draft	Rewrite paper using revision techniques. (Chapter 8)
7. Paper begins abruptly.	Introduction	Write an introduction that prepares readers for your paper. (Chapter 8)
8. Paper ends abruptly.	Conclusion	Write a conclusion that summarizes and/or suggests a new direction. (Chapter 8)
9. No connections among ideas.	Transitions	Go over paper and add transitions between parts of your paper. (Chapter 8)
10. Sentences are awkward, incomplete.	Sentence structure	Check to make sure your sentences are clear and complete. (Chapter 9)
11. Language is fuzzy.	Word choice, diction	Check to make sure that your language is clear and precise. (Chapter 6)
12. Problems with spelling, punctuation, and so on.	Mechanics	Go over paper and clear up surface errors. (Chapter 10)

Group Activity 2   *First Impressions*

Select a paper you have recently written but have not previously
shared. Exchange papers with another student and do a quick initial
reading of each other's work. Write out a brief analysis of the paper,
using the questions on pp. 119–120 and return both paper and analysis
to the other student.

   Now discuss with your partner what his or her initial reading indicates about your paper. Are you surprised by anything in your reader's
comments? Ask your reader to explain any comments you do not
understand.

   Write our your reaction to your reader's analysis and to your
discussion with the reader. How would you change the paper based on
your reader's comments? Do you see something about the paper that
you didn't see before? Keep both your reader's analysis and your reaction to it; you may want to use them later in this chapter.

Group Activity 3   *Description*

Using the same paper as was used for Group Activity 2, exchange papers with the same student who read your paper during that activity.
Write a description of each other's papers. Do not return either the
paper or the description. You will work with the paper again in the
next exercise.

Group Activity 4   *Evaluation*

Do an evaluation of the same paper you described in Group Activity 3.
Write a paragraph-by-paragraph evaluation and conclude it with a
summary.

   Remember the kinds of questions you're asking yourself as you
read this paper:

a. Is there a clear main idea in this paper?
b. Is there sufficient support and detail?
c. Are the ideas organized effectively? Can anything be cut or re-
   arranged?
d. Are language and sentence structure clear and complete?
e. Is the paper interesting?
f. Does the paper have a good introduction and conclusion?
g. Are there any parts of the paper that confuse me?

   Return the paper to the author when you have finished this
exercise.

Writing Activity 3   *Making Notes for Revision*

Review the evaluation which was done for your paper in Group Activity 4 on the preceding page. Make notes to guide you in revising your paper. You may need to refer to the "Notes for Revision" that were made on "Vandalism: A Serious Campus Problem" (p. 126). These notes may give you ideas for making your own notes.

Writing Activity 4   *Making a Rough Plan for Revision*

Using the evaluation of your paper in Group Activity 4 on the preceding page and the revision notes you made in Writing Activity 3 above, construct a rough plan for your paper. You may want to use the rough plan on p. 127 in this chapter to guide you.

Chapter 9
Revising Sentences and Words

In the preceding chapters, you have considered various ways to focus a paper, arrange ideas, and strengthen support. In this chapter, you will study a range of methods for structuring sentences and using words in a manner that conveys your intended meaning more effectively.

One way writers can convey meaning more effectively is by structuring sentences to show the relationships between the ideas they are discussing. Rather than presenting ideas one at a time, skilled writers combine related ideas within the same sentence. To see the usefulness of this kind of sentence combination, read each of the two versions of the following letter aloud:

Dear Mr. Rundles:

    My family purchased a Labrador retriever. We purchased it on June 15th of this year. It came from the Patterson branch of Beaumont Kennels. The dog was unsatisfactory from the beginning. This was unfortunate. Mr. Sandler was the salesman. He assured us that he would select the best puppy of the litter. The litter was champion-line. The puppies were born on April 13th. We saw the dog. We had our doubts. The pup seemed too large for being eight weeks old. Many of his features did not suggest champion lines. His coat should have been thick and black. It was thin and flecked with rust. He was far too squat for a Labrador retriever. We took the pup home. We tried to pet him. He hid behind the furniture. He refused food and water for more than a day. Later, we noticed his hoarse cough and watery eyes. We took him to a vet. The vet checked the pup. He checked him thoroughly. The vet gave us advice. We returned the dog to Mr. Sandler at the kennel. He refused to refund our payment. He would only give us credit toward another dog. We are asking you to help us get a full refund.

This version of the letter uses short simple sentences that do little to show connections between ideas. In the next version, the sentences have been revised to indicate these connections:

Dear Mr. Rundles:

On June 15th of this year, my family purchased a Labrador retriever from the Patterson branch of Beaumont Kennels. Unfortunately, the dog was unsatisfactory from the beginning. Mr. Sandler, the salesman, assured us that he would select the best puppy from a champion-line litter born April 13th. But when we saw the dog, we had our doubts. The pup seemed much too large, and many of his features did not suggest champion lines. For one thing, his coat, which should have been dense and black, was thin and flecked with rust. Also, he was far too squat for a Labrador retriever. After we got the pup home, he hid behind the furniture when we tried to pet him and refused food and water for more than a day. Later, we noticed his hoarse cough and watery eyes, so we took the dog to a vet, who checked him thoroughly. On the vet's advice, we returned the dog to Mr. Sandler at Beaumont Kennels, but he refused to refund our payment and would only give us credit toward another dog. We are asking you to help us get a full refund.

In the revised version, related ideas have been combined within the same sentence. As a result, the second version of the letter reads more smoothly and is much easier to understand.

Sentence-Combining Symbols

In this chapter, two symbols will be used to indicate the relationship between a full sentence and its parts.

A full sentence will be represented by a box:

Example: | **John went to the doctor.** |

A dependent word group (a string of related words that cannot be understood as a full sentence) will be represented by a wavy line: ～～～～

Example: **Because John felt sick**

Together these two symbols can quickly show the structure of a combined sentence:

〰〰〰〰〰〰〰, [＿＿＿＿＿＿＿].

Because John felt sick, he went to the doctor.

[＿＿＿＿＿＿＿] 〰〰〰〰〰〰〰.

John went to the doctor because he felt sick.

[＿], 〰〰〰〰〰〰〰, [＿＿＿＿＿＿].

John, because he felt sick, went to the doctor.

As you can see, dependent word groups can occur at the beginning, middle, or end of full sentences.

STRUCTURING SENTENCES FOR MEANING: COMBINING WHOLE SENTENCES

Sometimes, the information provided in two or more sentences might make better sense if it were all presented in a *single* sentence. For example, the four sentences below all pertain to a single incident:

The jetliner was a DC-10 with 143 passengers aboard.

The jetliner was taking off from the main runway.

It nearly collided with a small plane.

The small plane was crossing the runway after landing.

Because all these sentences relate to a common topic, they provide a variety of opportunities for combining pairs of sentences:

1. Combining Independent Sentences Using Coordinating Words: [＿＿＿＿], and [＿＿＿＿].

   The jetliner was taking off from the main runway, and it nearly collided with a small plane.

2. Combining Independent Sentences and Dependent Word Groups:

   a. By using subordinating words: 〰〰〰〰, [＿＿＿＿].

   As the jetliner was taking off from the main runway, it nearly collided with a small plane.

   b. By using relative pronouns: [＿＿＿＿] 〰〰〰.

   The jetliner nearly collided with a small plane that was crossing the runway after landing.

c. By adding phrases

The jetliner, a DC-10 with 143 passengers aboard, was taking off from the main runway.

Using the same techniques, it would also be possible to combine *all* of the sentences into one:

The jetliner, a DC-10 taking off from the main runway with 143 passengers aboard, nearly collided with a small plane that was crossing the runway after landing.

Each of these combined sentences emphasizes different aspects of the situation, making the relationship between ideas clearer and thus easier for the reader to understand. By using various ways to combine sentences during revision, you can make your writing much stronger.

Combining Independent Sentences Using Coordinating Words

The most common way to connect sentences is by using a link made up of a *comma* and a *coordinating word:*

Two sentences:

The building cost over $100 million. It was hideously ugly.

Combined sentence:

The building cost over $100 million, yet it was hideously ugly.

A sentence such as this is known as a *coordinate construction* because it coordinates two ideas that are balanced evenly on either side of the coordinating word.

Here are the most frequently used coordinating words, also known as coordinating conjunctions. Note that each word has a different meaning and sets up a specific relationship between two sentences.

and	(shows addition and sequence)
or	(shows an alternative)
but	(shows contrast)
for	(means "because")
so	(means "therefore")
yet	(means "on the other hand" or "nevertheless")

Examples:

and   It rained hard all night. By morning the streets were flooded.

It rained hard all night, *and* by morning the streets were flooded.

(The *and* shows the sequence of events.)

or   A bird might have struck the impeller blades of the jet engine. A fuel line might have burst.

A bird might have struck the impeller blades of the jet engine, *or* a fuel line might have burst.

(The word *or* shows alternative reasons for the problem that is implied.)

but   Roger claimed that he played chess. He couldn't even set up the board correctly.

Roger claimed that he played chess, *but* he couldn't even set up the board correctly.

(The word *but* shows the contrast between Roger's claim and what he could really do.)

for   We cleared away the brush all around the house. The fire danger was extreme.

We cleared away the brush all around the house, *for* the fire danger was extreme.

(The word *for* shows that the brush was cleared away *because* of the fire danger.)

so   The mess truck never showed up. We sent a squad to a nearby village to buy sausages and beer.

The mess truck never showed up, *so* we sent a squad to a nearby village to buy sausages and beer.

(The word *so* shows that because the mess truck never showed up, the squad went to the village to buy food and beer.)

yet   The cat had lost one leg after being struck by a car. It could still scramble over the low wall in the backyard.

The cat had lost one leg after being struck by a car, *yet* it could still scramble over the low wall in the backyard.

(The word *yet* shows that even though the cat lost a leg, *nevertheless* or *still*, it could scramble over the low wall.)

In the examples above, the coordinating conjunction clarifies the relationship between the ideas in each pair of sentences.

As you work through the exercises in this chapter, you may wish to compare your responses to those given in the answer key on pp. 237–244. Remember that in many exercises the sentences may be revised in a variety of ways; in such cases, there is no single correct answer.

Exercise 1 *Combining Sentences Using Coordinating Words*

Connect each pair of sentences with commas and coordinating words that show the relationship between the ideas expressed in each sentence. Choose the appropriate joining word from those given on pp. 141–142, and remember to use a comma before each coordinating word. You may find that some sentence pairs may be connected by one of several joining words.

> *Example:* The fern was overwatered. It quickly turned yellow.
>
> The fern was overwatered, and it quickly turned yellow.

1. She left to go to work. I stayed home to fix dinner.

   _____

   _____

2. The printer may be purchased with the computer. It may also be added to the system later.

   _____

   _____

3. The pilot whale was firmly beached in the shallow water near the jetty. It was still alive.

   _____

   _____

4. I was reluctant to have him work on my car. He seemed to have a careless attitude.

   _____

   _____

5. Her father died two months before she was born. She never knew him.

   _____

   _____

Exercise 2 *Revising Writing by Combining Sentences Using Coordinating Words*

Revise the following passage, connecting sentences wherever you feel this would make the writing easier to understand. Remember that clear connections make for clear meaning in any piece of writing. Afterward you may wish to compare your revision with another person's. This may demonstrate how the use of different joining words can change the meaning of a passage.

We left the car parked in the shade of a tree. We couldn't lock it because of the jammed window. We took along the camera. We locked the tape deck in the trunk. The day was overcast. It was hot. We began to sweat as soon as we started walking. I asked Susan how far it was to her aunt's cabin. I had never been there before. Susan said it was only about three quarters of a mile. It was all uphill. At least it seemed that way.

_____

_____

_____

_____

_____

_____

_____

_____

Combining Independent Sentences and Dependent Word Groups by Using Subordinating Words

As you have seen, coordinating words join sentences so that each remains complete and understandable:

Two sentences: ⬚. ⬚.

I was bored. I turned on the radio.

Combined sentence (using coordinating word):

⬚, so ⬚.

I was bored, so I turned on the radio.

Subordinating words work in a different fashion. A subordinating word *reduces* a sentence to one that is no longer complete and understandable. Notice, for example, what happens if we add the subordinating word *because* to a complete, understandable sentence:

Complete sentence: ⬚.

I was bored.

Incomplete sentence: 〰〰〰〰〰〰〰〰

Because I was bored

With the addition of the subordinating word the complete sentence becomes incomplete; it leaves us hanging, wanting to know what happened to the person who was bored. Because subordinating words have this effect, the expressions they introduce must always be joined to a complete sentence:

Combined sentence (using subordinating word):

〜〜〜〜〜〜〜〜〜〜〜〜, □□□□□□□□□□□□ .

Because I was bored, I turned on the radio.

Here are some important subordinating words; each indicates a different kind of logical relationship:

Subordinating Word	*Example*
if	*If* Bill can't go, Natasha will have to return the tickets.
unless	*Unless* the blockade is lifted, there is sure to be an epidemic.
although	*Although* cardiopulmonary resuscitation was attempted, the woman never regained consciousness.
because	The acid rain problem is becoming more severe *because* pollution from power plants is increasing.
since	The tombstone read: "*Since* your eyes closed, mine have not ceased to weep."
as	*As* the buzzer sounded, Traci hit on a twelve-foot jump shot.
when	*When* the last customer has left, we put the chairs on the tables and begin sweeping up.
before	*Before* the cease-fire was three hours old, more shelling began.
until	We can't leave *until* we hear from Lori.
while	*While* I was in junior high school, I seldom spoke to boys.

In using subordinating words, remember that if the combined sentence *begins* with a subordinate construction, this construction will usually be followed by a comma:

〜〜〜〜〜〜〜〜〜〜〜〜, □□□□□□□□□□□□ .

If Mike studies hard, he can pass the exam.

If the combined sentence *ends* with a subordinate construction, a comma is often not required:

Mike can pass the exam if he studies hard.

If the subordinate construction comes in the *middle* of the combined sentence, then *two* commas are needed:

Mike, if he studies hard, can pass the exam.

Exercise 3   *Combining Sentences with Subordinating Words*

Use subordinating words to join the following pairs of sentences. Try to suggest at least two revisions for each pair. In some cases you will need to make additional changes to the original sentence; see Example d.

Example:
The cotter pin broke.
The propeller sank.

a. When the cotter pin broke, the propeller sank.
b. Because the cotter pin broke, the propeller sank.
c. After the cotter pin broke, the propeller sank.
d. If the cotter pin breaks, the propeller will sink.

1. Interest rates fell.
   Stock prices soared.

   _____

   _____

2. The water in the goldfish bowl was not changed for two months.
   The goldfish all died.

   _____

   _____

3. The radar spotted an intruding aircraft.
   Fighters scrambled to intercept it.

   _____

   _____

4. The checks were inserted.
   The envelopes were taped shut.

   _____

   _____

5. The gymnast suffered a shoulder injury.
   She kept her scholarship.

   _____

   _____

Combining Independent Sentences and Dependent Word Groups by Using Relative Pronouns

A third way to combine sentences is by changing one sentence to a word group and inserting it within another sentence:

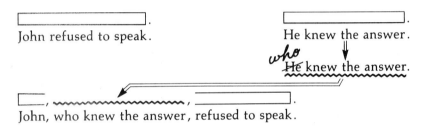

John refused to speak.

He knew the answer.

John, who knew the answer, refused to speak.

Notice how in this example the second sentence is reduced to a word group by changing "he" to "who." "Who" is one of a set of words called *relative pronouns*. They are called relative pronouns because they *relate* a word group to an appropriate word in the main part of the sentence. The arrows in the following sentences show how the relative pronoun makes this connection:

The new soft drink can, <u>which</u> was designed to attract children, looked as if it had been sprinkled with purple glitter.

Tran Thi Xuan, <u>who</u> was born in a village south of Saigon, escaped to Hong Kong when the communists took over South Vietnam.

Here are the most common relative pronouns, with an example sentence showing how each is used:

Relative Pronouns	*Example Sentences*
who	The second-string quarterback, *who* had never before started in a game, led the team to a win in the championship.

whom	Dana's father, *whom* I had never met, had the reputation of being very protective of his only daughter.
whose	Carolyn, *whose* paintings had earned her a scholarship at UCLA, opened a studio in Laguna Beach when she was only twenty-two.
which	The glue, *which* had probably been sitting on the shelf for twenty years, had dried into a solid, unusable mass.
that	The wine *that* was selected as best in the final testing was a fairly inexpensive Grey Riesling from a small winery in the Napa Valley.

Exercise 4   *Combining Sentences Using Relative Pronouns*

For each pair of sentences, reduce the italicized sentence to a word group by using the indicated relative pronoun, and then insert this word group into the other sentence at the point indicated by the ∧.

Examples:

Freud ∧ refused to take any medication except aspirin. *He suffered terrible pain from cancer of the jaw.* (Use *who.*)

> Freud, who suffered terrible pain from cancer of the jaw, refused to take any medication except aspirin.

The thruster ∧ was located in the nose of the orbiter. *It caused the problem.* (Use *that.*)

> The thruster that caused the problem was located in the nose of the orbiter.

For the last five sentence pairs you will need to make your own selection of the appropriate relative pronoun—who, whom, whose, which, or that.

1. The bridge ∧ finally collapsed. *It had been overloaded with truck traffic for years.* (Use *which.*)

———————————————————

———————————————————

2. Phillip ∧ had to quit school to take care of his mother. *He needed only fifteen more units to receive his degree.* (Use *who.*)

———————————————————

———————————————————

3. High-fat diets ∧ have been associated with increased risk of heart disease. *These diets are common in America.* (Use *which*.)

_____

_____

4. Tommy ∧ was not the most popular boy at the academy. *He had a habit of helping himself to other people's food.* (Use *who*.)

_____

_____

5. The fire ∧ was dead by morning. *It had not been tended during the night.* (Use *which*.)

_____

_____

6. The parents ∧ sat slumped against the far wall of the cabin. *Their boy was the only one still missing.* (Use *whose*.)

_____

_____

7. The hospital ∧ faces severe reductions under the terms of the new budget. *It is the sole provider of medical services for much of the inner-city population.* (Use *which*.)

_____

_____

8. My uncle ∧ cannot support himself on Social Security benefits. *He was forced to retire after his sixty-fifth birthday.* (Use an appropriate relative pronoun.)

_____

_____

9. The party ∧ continued for the entire Labor Day weekend. *It had gotten off to a slow start.* (Use an appropriate relative pronoun.)

_____

_____

10. My father ∧ broke into a rash whenever he entered the anatomy building. *He was highly allergic to formaldehyde.* (Use an appropriate relative pronoun.)

_____

_____

11. The home computer ʌ soon was causing squabbles over who could use it. *It had been purchased to solve problems.* (Use an appropriate relative pronoun.)

_____

_____

12. The small four-cylinder engine ʌ proved to be a winner when it was installed in the Lotus. *It had originally been designed to power farm machinery.* (Use an appropriate relative pronoun.)

_____

_____

Exercise 5   *Combining Sentences Using Relative Pronouns*

Construct *two* revised sentences from each of the following pairs. Follow the specific instructions for each revision.

Example: The pots had been sitting for a month in the sink. They were fully of fuzzy pink mold.

Revision 1:   Using *which*, add the second to the first:

The pots, *which were full of fuzzy pink mold,* had been sitting for a month in the sink.

Revision 2:   Using *which*, add the first to the second:

The pots, *which had been sitting for a month in the sink,* were full of fuzzy pink mold.

(Notice that in this revision, it was necessary to replace the subject of the second sentence—*they*—with that of the first sentence—*the pots.*)

A writer's choice of one revision over another depends on what meaning the writer intends to convey. The two revisions above have different meanings. In *Revision 1,* the writer's main point is that *the pots and pans had been sitting in the sink for a month.* In *Revision 2,* the writer wants to emphasize the point *that the pots were full of fuzzy pink mold.*

1. I had not seen Bianca for some time. She seemed thinner and grayer and even more beautiful.

*Revision 1: Using *who*, add the second to the first:

_____

_____

Revision 2: Using *whom,* add the first to the second:

_____

_____

2. The studio looked out over a wet garden full of bright new daffodils. The studio was rather barren.

   Revision 1: Using *which,* add the second to the first:

   _____

   _____

   Revision 2: Using *which,* add the first to the second:

   _____

   _____

3. The child stood clutching her father's legs. She could not have been older than four.

   Revision 1: Using *who,* add the second to the first:

   _____

   _____

   Revision 2: Using *who,* add the first to the second:

   _____

   _____

4. The cut ran down her thumb and across her palm. It required more than thirty stitches to close.

   Revision 1: Using *which,* add the second to the first:

   _____

   _____

   Revision 2: Using *which,* add the first to the second:

   _____

   _____

5. The lecturer was a well-known bore. He continued to talk at the audience for another forty minutes.

   Revision 1: Using *who,* add the second to the first:

   _____

   _____

   Revision 2: Using *who,* add the first to the second:

   _____

   _____

Exercise 6   *Modifying Sentences with Relative Pronouns*

Using relative pronouns (*who, whom, whose, which, that*), add modifying ideas of your own choice to the following sentences. Make *two* revisions for each sentence, noting the different meaning suggested by each revision.

> *Example:*   The physician looked discouraged and exhausted.
>
> *Revision 1:*   The physician, *who had just gotten out of surgery*, looked discouraged and exhausted.
>
> *Revision 2:*   The physician, *whom I had never seen before*, looked discouraged and exhausted.

1. Miss Millet was my teacher in first grade.

   _____

   _____

   _____

   _____

2. The football team was confident.

   _____

   _____

   _____

   _____

3. The dinner was no longer edible.

   _____

   _____

   _____

   _____

4. The train caught fire.

   _____

   _____

   _____

   _____

Combining Independent Sentences and Dependent Word Groups by Adding Phrases

It is sometimes possible to reduce one sentence to a key word or phrase, which can then be *added* to a second sentence:

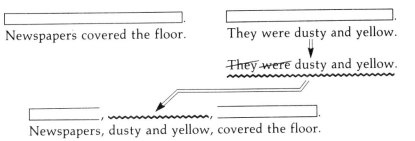

This technique is especially helpful when the sentence to be reduced contains only a small bit of useful information and a large number of unnecessary words. As the following examples show, the added phrases can take a variety of forms:

> *original:* Doug was headstrong and would never admit to a mistake. His father had been headstrong, too.
>
> *revision:* Doug was headstrong, like his father, and would never admit to a mistake.
>
> *original:* She acted quickly. She threw out a lifebuoy and brought the boat about.
>
> *revision:* Acting quickly, she threw out a lifebuoy and brought the boat about.
>
> *original:* Jamie was a very determined young lady. She was an expert at bluffing her playmates.
>
> *revision:* Jamie, a very determined young lady, was an expert at bluffing her playmates.

Exercise 7   *Adding Phrases*

For each of the sentence pairs below, reduce the italicized sentence to a word or phrase and add it to the other sentence. The sentence pairs are arranged in four groups; use the example given for each group as a model for that section.

> *Example A*
>
> *original:*   We slept on the beach. *We were cold and tired.*
>
> *revision:*   Cold and tired, we slept on the beach.

1. *The key was thick with rust.* The key would no longer fit the lock.

   _____

   _____

2. The cheese had a rotten smell. *It was soft and overripe.*

   _____

   _____

3. The baby'e eyes were severely infected. *They were oozy and red.*

   _____

   _____

4. *The meadow was full of round white rocks.* It was nearly a quarter-mile wide at this point.

   _____

   _____

5. The mayfly was trapped in the surface film of the pond. *She was heavy with eggs.*

   _____

   _____

   Example B

   original: Our scoutmaster knew how to use a map and compass. *He was a retired merchant marine officer.*

   revision: Our scoutmaster, a retired merchant marine officer, knew how to use a map and compass.

6. The bus driver is always willing to answer questions about routes and transfers. *He is a patient man.*

   _____

   _____

7. Sandra never made it to shore. *She was a poor swimmer.*

   _____

   _____

8. His father still takes long bicycle trips each weekend. *He was a member of the U.S. cycling team at the 1952 Olympics.*

   _____

   _____

9. *Rhonda is a frequent visitor to Mexico.* She loves to bargain with the shopkeepers.

   _____

   _____

10. My roommate never throws anything away. *She is a real pack rat.*

    _____

    _____

Example C

original: We had trouble finding a place to stay in Salzburg. *We arrived after midnight.*

revision: Having arrived after midnight, we had trouble finding a place to stay in Salzburg.

11. *We lifted up the lid.* We peered inside.

    _____

    _____

12. *The fullback swept to the left.* He made a seven-yard gain.

    _____

    _____

13. *The gull dove suddenly.* It snapped up a fish.

    _____

    _____

14. The fire threatened a convalescent hospital. *The fire was still burning out of control.*

    _____

    _____

15. *The two men were arguing loudly.* They disappeared down the street.

    _____

    _____

Example D

original: I finally sold the car to a mechanic who wanted to race it. *I didn't sell the spare engine, however.*

revision: I finally sold the car, without the spare engine, to a mechanic who wanted to race it.

16. We moved back to Cincinnati. *This was in the spring.*

_____

_____

17. The prime minister eventually agreed to lift the trade restrictions. *He did this under pressure from the U.S. State Department.*

_____

_____

18. He began going to the quarterhorse races every night. *He started this after his birthday.*

_____

_____

19. The truck broke down within twenty miles. *It was in poor repair.*

_____

_____

20. All students must pass a comprehensive writing exam. *They must pass it before graduating.*

_____

_____

Exercise 8   *Revising with Reduced Sentences*

Revise the following passage, using the techniques you have practiced in the previous exercise.

The mill stands on the south side of Jedadiah Creek. It is a two-story structure. It is L-shaped. The roof is thatched. It is steeply pitched. The roof needs repairs. The chestnut tree has thrust an arm through it. The walls are solidly timbered. They looked as if they could last another two centuries. The waterwheel continues to slowly revolve. It is dappled with green patches of moss. It empties one bucket after another back into the millstream.

_____

_____

_____

_____

_____

_____

_____

_____

_____

Writing Activity 1   *Reducing Sentences in Your Writer's Notebook*

Find several places in your Writer's Notebook that might benefit from this kind of reduce-and-add revision. Make the revisions on the page. There is no need to recopy the revised sentence.

Exercise 9   *Revising a Passage by Combining Sentences*

The passage below is difficult to read and understand because it contains many short, choppy sentences that don't show relationships between the ideas in those sentences. Revise the passage by combining some of these sentences using coordinating words, subordinating words, relative pronouns, or added phrases.

Coordinating Words	*Subordinating Words*	*Relative Pronouns*
and	if	who
but	unless	whom
or	although	whose
for	because	which
so	since	that
yet	as	
	when	
	after	
	before	
	during	
	until	
	while	

    Franz Ferdinand was the crown prince of Austria. He was assassinated on June 28, 1914. He was visiting the town of Sarajevo. Franz Ferdinand entered the town riding in an open car at the head of the procession. The first assassination attempt was made with a bomb. The bomb was accurately thrown. Franz Ferdinand deflected it with his arm. The bomb exploded behind the car. This incident was unnerving. Franz Ferdinand refused to cancel the visit. Security was lax. Army troops were available to line the parade route. They were not used. Their uniforms were not impressive enough. The procession continued down the road. Franz Ferdinand's driver missed a turn. He had to back up. A second assassin was standing nearby. He walked up to the car. He fired two shots. Franz Ferdinand was hit once in the neck. He bled to death within a few minutes. His last words were, "It is nothing." His assassination helped to trigger World War I.

_____

_____

_____

_____

_____

_____

_____

_____

_____

_____

_____

_____

_____

_____

_____

_____

Writing Activity 2   *Using Subordinate Constructions to Revise Your Own Writing*

Read through discovery drafts or your writer's notebook, looking for sentences to join using subordinate constructions. Add the appropriate subordinating conjunction or relative pronoun and make any other necessary changes. You do not need to recopy the entire passage. Find at least ten sentences to revise in this manner. Make sure the joined sentences make the meaning clearer by showing relationships between ideas.

STRENGTHENING SENTENCES FOR MEANING

Consider the following statement, which the mayor of a large city made about solving this city's problems:

The solution is in the hands of the people, and we will never succeed as responsible citizens unless we go into the minds and hearts of the people and stand side by side to confront any problems we have to solve.

It is difficult to figure out what the mayor wants the people to do. Now consider the following statement:

> This city has an antiquated sewer system, which must be replaced. If we want to stop raw sewage from seeping into our water supply, we must vote for a new sewer system and be willing to pay for it with increased taxes.

The meaning of the second statement is clear.

The mayor may have been deliberately vague in the first statement in order to avoid losing votes—you almost never hear a local politician mention the words "increased taxes." Such vague writing is safe and easy for the writer, but as you can see, it has very little meaning for the reader. In the second statement, specific words that convey a precise meaning have replaced the vague language of the first statement.

As you rethink and revise your writing, you can strengthen your sentences in two ways:

1. Expanding: adding words and phrases that help get your meaning across to the reader

2. Tightening: getting rid of unnecessary words and phrases that just confuse or distract your reader.

The exercises in this section will help you learn the techniques you need to strengthen your sentences.

Expanding Sentences

Your early drafts may capture main or general ideas but lack the convincing detail needed to support these ideas. We discussed this need for support in Chapter 4, where you worked on providing adequate examples, facts, details, reasons, and incidents to back up your ideas. In the exercises below we'll show you how to provide supporting detail by using specific words and by adding words or word groups to sentences.

Making Words Specific. This is one way to help your readers understand what you are saying in a sentence. Consider these two sentences:

The man looked at the dog.	The general terms *man* and *dog* may not give readers enough information.
The burglar looked at the Doberman pinscher.	The specific words *burglar* and *Doberman pinscher* give readers more information.

Now look at these sentences:

The man walked down the
street.

The man stumbled down the   The word *stumbled* gives a
street.   reader a more specific mental
                                 picture than the word *walked*.

The man hurried down the   Note that changing *stumbled* to
street.   *hurried* completely changes the
                                 meaning of the sentence.

When revising, think about whether you need to make general
words more specific to ensure that your readers understand your
meaning.

Exercise 10   *Making Words Specific*

In each of the sentences below, replace the italicized words with specific
words. Do two different revisions for each sentence and observe how
the meaning changes.

1. This *place* has *problems.*

   _____

   _____

2. The *person drank* the *beverage.*

   _____

   _____

3. I am allergic to *many things.*

   _____

   _____

4. His *vehicle* needs *work.*

   _____

   _____

5. My refrigerator is filled with *food.*

   _____

   _____

6. We regularly watch *certain television shows.*

   _____

   _____

7. The police officer *talked to* the *man*.

_____

_____

Adding Descriptive Words and Word Groups to Sentences. Sentences can often be improved by adding words and word groups that give the reader a clearer picture of what is happening in the sentence. As you write, you have a mental picture of any person, place, or thing you wish to describe. You must give readers enough details and information so that they can share your mental picture. Consider these sentences:

The job applicant wore a suit.

The job applicant wore a *cheap* suit.

Adding *cheap* gives the reader a better idea of the job applicant's appearance and also changes the meaning of the sentence.

The job applicant wore a *cheap* suit, a *frayed tie*, and *scuffed shoes*.

If the job applicant's appearance is important to the meaning the writer wants to convey, then these details could be added. (They might support the idea that the job applicant needs work desperately.)

The job applicant waited.

Smoking nervously, the job applicant waited.

The job applicant *smoked nervously and paced up and down the hall* as he waited.

This information about how the job applicant acted and where he was gives the reader a clear mental picture and provides further support for the idea that the job applicant needs work desperately.

Sometimes writers use words and word groups that do not give readers a clear mental picture. Consider the following sentences:

That car is really great looking.

It's pretty as a picture.

It's dynamite.

It's super looking.

From these sentences, readers may get the idea that this car is attractive, but they would have no image of the specific car the writer is describing. *Really* and *great* are vague words; *pretty as a picture* is a cliché (an overused expression); *dynamite* and *super* are examples of slang (informal language that is often used by just one age or social group and usually goes out of date quickly).

You may occasionally decide that a slang expression or cliché is clear and adds color and life to your sentence. Usually, however, you should replace such language with more specific words or word groups as you revise.

Group Activity 1   *Expanding Sentences*

Below are two short sentences. The model on the left illustrates how you can add detail. Using the revision of the sentence in the left column as your guide, revise the sentence in the right column by making words more specific and by adding words and word groups as indicated.

Model Sentence	*Your Sentence*
The woman sued the paper.	The person got rid of the car.

Making words more specific

The actress sued the *National Enquirer*.	_____ _____

Adding words

The actress *promptly* sued the *National Enquirer*.	_____ _____

Adding word groups—1

The actress, *a serious contender for an Academy Award,* promptly sued the *National Enquirer*.	_____ _____

Adding word groups—2

The actress, a serious contender for an Academy Award, promptly sued the *National Enquirer for printing stills from her unreleased film.*	_____ _____ _____

Adding word groups—3

The actress, a serious contender for an Academy Award, promptly sued the *National Enquirer* for printing stills from her unreleased film, *Return of the Swamp Woman.*	_____ _____ _____

Group Activity 2   *Expanding Sentences*

Again, use the revisions of the sentence in the left column as your model for revisions of the sentence on the right. Notice how your sentence grows in detail and gathers meaning as you make the words more specific and add words and word groups. You may rarely write sentences this long, but this exercise helps you see the possibilities for sentence expansion.

Model Sentence	*Your Sentence*
The man ate the food.	The student left the class.

Making words more specific

Garth wolfed down the *sandwich.*   _____

_____

Adding words

Garth *hungrily* wolfed down   _____
the *salami* sandwich.
                                                      _____

Adding word groups—1

Garth, *who had been on a*   _____
diet for a week, hungrily wolfed
down the salami sandwich.   _____

                                                      _____

Adding word groups—2

Garth, who had been on a   _____
water diet for a week,
hungrily wolfed down the   _____
salami sandwich *from the corner*
deli.   _____

Adding word groups—3

Garth, who had been on a   _____
water diet for a week,
hungrily wolfed down the   _____
salami sandwich from the
corner deli *before he got back*   _____
home.
                                                      _____

Exercise 11   *Expanding Sentences*

Revise *five* of the sentences below by making words more specific and adding words and word groups.

1. The man spoke to the woman.

   _____

   _____

2. The politician reported on the situation.

   _____

   _____

3. The woman greeted her relative.

   _____

   _____

4. The business failed.

   _____

   _____

5. The band began to play.

   _____

   _____

6. The workers went on strike.

   _____

   _____

7. The family gathered.

   _____

   _____

8. The team left the field.

   _____

   _____

9. The girl fell.

   _____

   _____

10. The waiter brought the meal.

   _____

   _____

Your instructor may ask you to share some of your revisions from this exercise.

Exercise 12   *Revising a Paragraph*

Revise the following paragraph by making words more specific and by adding words and word groups that clarify meaning.

> The trip was a disaster. We slept too late, which caused problems from the start. We forgot some important things. Denise and John got into an argument. We took a wrong turn. Just before we got back to the road we should have been on, we ran out of gas. John walked to a gas station. When he got back, we couldn't find the spout to the gas can, so we had problems transferring the fuel. By this time it was noon, so we stopped at a little place for lunch. The service was slow and the food was cold. When we got back on the road, it started to rain and one of the windshield wipers wouldn't work right. We stopped to fix it and I got very wet. By the time we arrived at the cabins, it was very late. We had to wake up the manager. He was not very pleasant, but then neither were we by that time.

_____

_____

_____

_____

_____

_____

_____

_____

_____

_____

Your instructor may ask you to share some of your revisions from this exercise.

Writing Activity 3   *Adding Support by Expanding Sentences*

1. Read through your Writer's Notebook entries or papers you have written, and select one or two passages containing ideas that need more support if your reader is to understand your meaning.

2. Revise these passages, supporting your ideas more convincingly by making words specific and by adding words or word groups to individual sentences.

Tightening Sentences

Unrevised writing is apt to contain unnecessary words and phrases that confuse or distract a reader.

Removing Padding and Deadwood. In revising your writing, look for padding or deadwood, words and phrases that are not needed and can be cut with no loss of meaning. Consider this example:

> At the present time, the state of California is actively involved in the process of developing evacuation procedures to be employed in the possible event of nuclear emergency.

Can you recognize the deadwood in this sentence? How many words could be eliminated without a loss of meaning? If you underlined the essential words, the sentence might look like this:

> At the present time, the state of <u>California</u> <u>is</u> in the process of <u>developing</u> <u>evacuation procedures</u> to be employed in the possible event of <u>nuclear emergency</u>.

Using these essential words as the base for a revised sentence, you might come up with this:

> California is developing evacuation procedures for nuclear emergency.

Twenty-eight words have become eight, and a fuzzy sentence has become clearer.

Exercise 13   *Getting Rid of Deadwood*

Underline the essential words and phrases in the sentences below, and then rewrite the sentences to express the ideas more precisely.

1. It is my belief that it is of great importance for the college student to set up a schedule that involves studying on a regular basis in order to get assignments in on time when they are due, and especially long-term projects.

   _____

   _____

2. My future plans involve a very extended trip over a period of time with a close personal friend of mine.

   _____

   _____

3. In my opinion, there are a number of reasons why I think we don't really need to consider going during the month of January.

_____

_____

4. After careful thought I have come to the final conclusion that at this time we have more than enough natural resources and alternative fuel supplies to overcome the supposedly threatening energy crisis.

_____

_____

_____

Writing Activity 4   *Getting Rid of Deadwood*

Choose five sentences from your papers or Writer's Notebook entries. Underline the essential words and phrases, the ones you must keep to get your meaning across. Are there words that could be cut with no loss of meaning? Remove the deadwood and rewrite the sentence so that every word counts.

Tightening IT IS and THERE ARE Sentences. Most writers overuse IT IS and THERE ARE sentences. These sentences begin with *it is, it was, there is, there was, there are, there were,* or similar forms. Sometimes, of course, such sentences say just what you mean: "It is raining." Often, however, the IT IS or THERE ARE construction contributes almost nothing to what the sentence means:

> *original:* There were three problems that delayed the flight of the space shuttle.
>
> *revision:* Three problems delayed the flight of the space shuttle.

IT IS and THERE ARE sentences are easy to revise. Ask yourself whether the removal of the IT IS or THERE ARE construction significantly changes the meaning of the sentence. If the answer is no, you are probably correct in making the change. Line out the IT IS or THERE ARE and then read the sentence to see if anything else needs to be cut:

> ~~There were~~ three problems that delayed the flight of the space shuttle.

The *that* must also be removed to make a good sentence:

> ~~There were~~ three problems ~~that~~ delayed the flight of the space shuttle.

Sometimes you will also need to play with the order of the revised sentence:

~~It was~~ the shaving lotion ~~that~~ I was allergic to.

I was allergic to the shaving lotion.

Exercise 14   *Revising IT IS and THERE ARE Constructions*

Revise the following IT IS and THERE ARE constructions. In some instances you will have to make major changes in order to produce a sensible revision. You may decide that some sentences are clearer without revision.

1. It was late in the afternoon when Mandy arrived.

   _____

   _____

2. There were two children playing basketball in the school yard.

   _____

   _____

3. There is a complex chemical process that causes trees to shed their leaves.

   _____

   _____

4. There was a muffled knocking sound that the engine always made until the car was thoroughly warmed up.

   _____

   _____

5. It is hot in this room.

   _____

   _____

Writing Activity 5   *Tightening IT IS and THERE ARE Sentences*

Read through your Writer's Notebook entries and your papers, looking for sentences that use unnecessary IT IS and THERE ARE constructions. Revise five of these sentences.

Tightening Passive Sentences. Most sentences in English are *active;* that is, the subject of the sentence is also the doer of the action. (See pp. 177–178 for help in identifying subjects.)

Active Sentence	*Subject/Doer*	*Action*
The chemical companies polluted the river.	chemical companies	polluted

Some sentences are *passive:* the subject of the sentence is acted upon.

Passive Sentence	*Subject*	*Action*	*Doer*
The river had been polluted by the chemical companies.	river	had been polluted	chemical companies

A passive sentence is necessary if the doer of an action is unknown, or if the writer does not want to indicate who is responsible for an action.

Passive Sentence	*Subject*	*Action*	*Doer*
The river has been polluted.	river	has been polluted	(unknown)
A decision to fire six people has been made.	decision	has been made	(not indicated)

Passive sentences are usually longer and less clear than active sentences. Compare the following two sentences:

passive: Martha was fired by John.
active: John fired Martha.

To change unnecessary passive sentences into active ones, determine who is the doer of the action and make that doer the subject of the revised sentence. In the example above, John, the doer of the action, becomes the subject of the revised sentence.

Exercise 15   *Tightening Passive Sentences*

Tighten the following sentences by changing them from passive to active.

1. The accident was caused by the captain.

2. The body was discovered by the night custodian.

_____

3. Inexperienced workers are not hired by the company.

_____

4. The bait was taken by the trout.

_____

5. The organization of the quality control unit was immediately changed by the new manager.

_____

_____

Writing Activity 5   *Finding Passive Sentences in Your Own Writing*

Look through your Writer's Notebook and papers and find five passive sentences. Revise any of the sentences that would be clearer if you made them active.

Part II

Resources

Chapter 10
*Identifying and Correcting Errors*_____

- Putting Errors in Perspective
- Error Correction Log and Skills Check
    - Keeping Track of Mistakes
    - Skills Check
- Repairing Sentences
    - Identifying Complete Sentences
    - Identifying and Correcting Incomplete Sentences
    - Identifying and Correcting Run-Together Sentences
    - Identifying and Correcting Nonparallel Sentences
    - Identifying and Correcting Verb Problems
    - Identifying and Correcting Pronoun Problems
- Punctuation Skills
    - Commas
    - Semicolons
    - Colons
    - Dashes
    - Parentheses
    - Hyphens
    - Quotation Marks
    - Setting Off Titles
    - Forming Contractions with Apostrophes
    - Showing Possession
    - Capitals
    - Numbers
- Troublesome Words
- Spelling Skills

PUTTING ERRORS IN PERSPECTIVE

Many people believe that good writing means *not* making mistakes in grammar or punctuation. This is only partially correct. As we have suggested throughout this book, effective writing requires that the writer explore the topic in depth, express a clear main idea, provide adequate support, and revise thoroughly. The writer who neglects these major parts of the writing process will not produce a very strong paper even if it contains no errors at all.

But good writing—writing that is well thought out and properly developed—will always be weakened by errors in grammar and punctuation, and this is why you need to be able to recognize and correct mechanical flaws. These kinds of mistakes harm your writing in two ways:

> They may distract or confuse your reader.
>
> They give the reader the wrong impression about you and your writing. If your writing is full of small errors, the reader may distrust or discredit your ideas.

For these reasons, you need to know how to deal with sentence-level errors in your writing.

The *wrong* way to handle errors is to be overly concerned with them early in the writing process. Nothing disrupts the writing process as much as trying to avoid making any errors. If you worry too much about making mistakes, you may be unable to focus on what you want to say in your writing.

The *right* way to deal with errors is to realize that they are a natural part of the writing process. All writers make mistakes. Good writers learn to recognize and correct them during revision. In this chapter we will suggest techniques that will help you recognize and correct your own errors.

The Answer Key for the exercises in this chapter is on pp. 247–259.

ERROR CORRECTION LOG AND SKILLS CHECK

Keeping Track of Mistakes

The best way to improve your punctuation and grammar skills is to concentrate on one or two *selected* problems at a time, rather than to try to eliminate all your errors at once. You can help yourself do this by keeping an error correction log:

1. Based upon the skills check given below and your instructor's corrections on early papers, review the kinds of mistakes you are in the

habit of making. Select those problems you most want to eliminate, but don't try to handle more than two or three types of errors at once. If you tend to make the same kind of error many times in a paper, then focus *only* on that one kind of mistake.

2. Set aside a special part of your Writer's Notebook as an error correction log. In this log, keep track of the errors you have chosen to concentrate upon. For each assignment after you begin to keep the log, record the kind of error, the number of times it occurs in the assignment, and a correct revision of each occurrence. You may also wish to record notes or tips about how to correct the error. A section of an error correction log would look something like this:

Assignment	Error	Number of Occurrences	Correction and Comments
Paper 3	Run-together sentence	2	That's not anything new. I think most mothers feel that way. (Corrected with a period)
			She bought my first violin, and she paid for my music lessons. (Joined with a comma and an *and*)
	-s ending on verb	1	She still comes to every performance.

3. Review your error correction log before doing a final revision of any paper. This will remind you of problems to look for and ways to correct them.

4. When you have mastered one kind of problem and it no longer shows up on your log, replace it with another and begin to concentrate on eliminating that error as well.

Skills Check

The student paper on p. 176 has been altered so that it contains a number of mechanical errors. As a check of your own error-correction skills, read through the essay, revising anything that seems incorrect. Make your corrections on the draft itself.

When you have finished correcting the paper, compare your revision with the corrected version given on pp. 247. Then, in the spaces provided below, list any kind of error that you did not identify or that you corrected improperly.

_____	_____
_____	_____
_____	_____
_____	_____

This list can serve as a basis for selecting the two or three kinds of problems that you will want to begin concentrating upon in your error correction log.

My First Job

I folded the newspaper neatly and wrap a rubber band around it so that it would not fly open when I threw them on the porch. When I had finished wrapping all sixty newspapers. I loaded them on my little red wagon and started to distribute them to my customers. It was not a hard job, it was not an easy one either.

One of the hard parts was delivering in the wintertime when the temperature dropped below freezing and the snow was two to three feet deep, Too deep to walk in. I wear thick clothing, usually more than two layers. Even though I could keep my body warm, my face would froze. After being outside for a while my face would become numb from the chilly air. Pulling the wagon through the thick snow was tough. Most of the time I would have to leave my wagon at a corner pick up several newspapers distribute them and then pulling the wagon through the next block.

The cold was not the only difficulty. I had to be on the alert constantly for dogs. Usually people did not let their dogs out in the wintertime, in the summertime various sizes of dogs roam the streets, posing great problems for paper boys and mailmen.

Another problem that i had to deal with was collecting money at the end of the week. Most people paid on time, but there some who would delay his payments for as long as four weeks. It was really annoying finding them not at home. Or hearing them say that they would have the money in a week or two. Usually I would not wrap rubber bands around their newspapers—not until they had paid the bill.

Despite all of these problems; delivering newspapers was a good experience. I learned a lot about people and how to deal with them, I also learned to handle money properly and to take responsibilities. It was a good start for me in learning about life.

REPAIRING SENTENCES

This section shows how to identify and correct the most common kinds of sentence errors: incomplete sentences, run-together sentences, and nonparallel sentences.

Identifying Complete Sentences

In order to mend incorrect sentences, you must first be able to tell the difference between sentences and nonsentences. Two methods, or tests, may be used to identify sentences.

The Complete-Idea Test for Sentences.   As a speaker of a language, you probably have greater grammatical knowledge of that language than you give yourself credit for. For one thing, speakers of a language can recognize what is or is not a sentence in the language. You can apply this knowledge to your writing simply by reading your written sentences *aloud* and asking yourself whether they are complete. For example, consider how you would respond if someone spoke the following words to you:

I feel happy.

You would probably wonder about the cause of the person's happiness, and you might wonder why he or she chose to inform you of it, but you would at least understand one fairly complete idea: the person claims to be happy.

Compare your response to *I feel happy* with the way you react to the following words:

When I feel happy.

These words leave you hanging; you don't know *what* the person does when he or she feels happy. This sense of being left hanging often indicates that a sentence is incomplete.

Your ability to distinguish complete sentences from incomplete sentences is something that you share with all speakers of the language, and something that you can use to check and improve the sentences you write. To see how this ability can be used, read each of the following word groups aloud. As you do so, ask yourself whether the words express a complete idea or leave you hanging. Then check the explanation beneath each word group to see how it compares with your own.

Note: Here, as in Chapter 9, the box symbol (☐) is used to indicate a complete sentence, and the wavy-line symbol (〜〜〜) is used to indicate an incomplete sentence.

She was painting the fence.

☐ . Even though we don't know who "she" is, we still have a complete idea of what is happening.

Painting the fence.

～～～ This leaves us hanging. We do not know who did the painting or when the painting was done.

In the beginning Robert enjoyed the class.

☐. Even though we don't know which class Robert enjoyed, we still understand the complete idea that he did enjoy some class.

In the beginning.

～～～ This leaves us hanging. We don't know who is involved or what is happening "in the beginning."

Sarah drove to the bank. After lunch.

☐. ～～～ The first word group is a complete sentence, but the second is not. Even though "after lunch" makes sense in terms of the preceding sentence, *by itself* it is incomplete and leaves us hanging.

Exercise 1   *Identifying Complete Sentences by Using the Complete-Idea Test*

Use the complete-idea test to determine which of the following word groups are complete sentences. Read each word group aloud and ask yourself if it expresses a complete idea or leaves you hanging.

If the word group is a complete sentence, draw a box around it:

LaRhonda took the call.

If the word group is not a complete sentence, mark it with a wavy line and explain *why* it leaves you hanging:

Stopped ticking.

This leaves me hanging because I don't know *what* stopped ticking. It might have been a watch or a clock (or a bomb), but I can't tell.

1. A policeman drove us around the huge parking lot looking for the car.

   _____

   _____

2. And to the Fourth of July picnic in Crescent City, which was best of all.

   _____

   _____

3. Although I called several times and even left a note in the screen door.

_____

_____

4. My cat hates windy days.

_____

_____

5. She staring at the floor for a long time.

_____

_____

6. Dropped it on the deck.

_____

_____

7. Which was why we didn't get along.

_____

_____

8. Asking if I was sure that I'd done the job right.

_____

_____

9. The whole afternoon was wasted.

_____

_____

10. Because I had already proven myself working as an intern in the blueprint department during the summer.

_____

_____

The Subject-Verb Test for Sentences. This method for identifying sentences is based on the idea that all sentences contain two parts: a subject part and a verb part.

The <u>subject</u> tells *who* or *what:*

Who: <u>Eric</u> surfs.
Who: <u>Witches</u> cast spells.

What: The hailstones ruined the paint job on my car.
What: Jogging before breakfast wakes me up.

The verb part tells what the subject *does, is,* or *has:*

Does: The American people elect their president.
Does: I will keep my car in the garage.
Is: Sam is a trucker.
Is: Drinking coffee was my one bad habit.
Has: Andrea has a 3.5 grade point average.
Has: People in shopping malls have a greedy look.

If a word group cannot be divided into a subject part and a verb part, then it is not a complete sentence:

Jogging after breakfast makes me sick. (Complete sentence.)

Video games are ruining my life. (Complete sentence.)

The puzzle will keep them busy. (Complete sentence.)

Jogging after breakfast. (Incomplete sentence. Nothing *does, is,* or *has.*)

Video games. (Incomplete sentence. Nothing *does, is,* or *has.*)

Will keep them busy. (Incomplete sentence. We don't know *who* or *what* will keep them busy.)

Jump! (Complete sentence. This appears to have no subject, but actually the subject is an understood *you,* as in "You jump!")

Exercise 2   *Identifying Complete Sentences by Using the Subject-Verb Test*

Identify the complete sentences and incomplete sentences among the following word groups by using the subject-verb test. For each word group, underline the subject once and the verb part twice. Explain what part is missing in any incomplete sentences you discover.

1. In the river on the last day of school.

2. The foxes sitting beside the log.

_____

3. Soft drinks rot teeth.

_____

4. Maude, who dislikes children.

_____

5. Sat down and cried.

_____

6. Poetry is a mystery to me.

_____

7. Especially Halloween and Christmas.

_____

8. I attended every class.

_____

9. The theory that the sun, not the earth, is the center of the solar system.

_____

10. That he get out of her life.

_____

Exercise 3   *Constructing Complete Sentences*

Construct complete sentences by selecting a subject part from the list on the left and matching it with one of the verb parts on the right. Copy your completed sentences on the blank lines.

Subject Part

1. Correct braking techniques
2. As the curtain rose on the darkened stage, a hush
3. The povery and deprivation of his childhood, things he never talked openly about,
4. Swimming
5. Graciously extending her hand, the mayor
6. Long ago though it was, the scandal caused by the Chicago White Sox in the 1919 World Series

Verb Part

a. walked toward her defeated opponent
b. are nutritious snacks.
c. swept across the audience.
d. influenced the kind of adult he became.
e. is a sport in which an amateur is unlikely to suffer injuries.
f. help prevent skidding, even in panic stops.
g. is still controversial.

Subject Part

7. He
8. Films such as *Hearts and Minds* (1974), *The Deer Hunter* (1978), *Coming Home* (1978), and *Platoon* (1986)
9. The reaction of most parents to groups such as the Beastie Boys
10. Peanuts, almonds, raisins, and sunflower seeds

Verb Part

h. straightened his tie, took a deep breath, and walked briskly into the courtroom.
i. helped shape the American public's image of the Vietnam War.
j. is easy to predict.

Identifying and Correcting
Incomplete Sentences

Incomplete sentences may be identified using either of the methods discussed in the previous section. An incomplete sentence does not express a *complete idea*, and it does not contain *both* a subject and a verb.

Incomplete sentences may sometimes be corrected by adding an appropriate subject or verb part to complete the meaning:

Enjoyed the date festival.

This word group leaves the reader hanging; it is not a complete sentence.

I enjoyed the date festival.

Adding the subject I is one way to make this a complete sentence.

During revision, you may find that an incomplete sentence belongs with one of the sentences next to it. In such cases the incomplete sentence may be mended by attaching it to the appropriate adjacent sentence:

I have always done my best work in hard technical classes. Especially chemistry and math.

The second word group is an incomplete sentence. Although it begins with a capital letter and ends with a period, it is not a sentence.

I have always done my best work in hard technical classes, especially chemistry and math.

In the revision, the incomplete sentence has been attached to the sentence before it with a comma.

Exercise 4   *Identifying and Correcting Incomplete Sentences*
Revise the following paragraph by identifying and correcting any incomplete sentences within it. Some of the incomplete sentences may be attached to adjacent sentences. Others may require the addition of an appropriate subject or verb part.

She sat before the window. Rigid and still like a cat waiting for a mouse. The clock ticked in the darkened hallway. And finally startled her when it chimed out the hour. Two o'clock. Turned on the light. She shook her head. And shuffled off to the kitchen. Where she opened the refrigerator door. A note was inside.

_____
_____
_____
_____
_____
_____
_____
_____
_____

Identifying and Correcting Run-Together Sentences

Run-together sentences are just the reverse of incomplete sentences: instead of containing too little, they contain too much. A run-together sentence jams two or more sentences into a form meant to express only one:

The spacecraft malfunctioned the mission was aborted.

Run-together sentences can be corrected in one of four ways:

1. Divide the run-together sentence by using a *period.*

   The spacecraft malfunctioned. The mission was aborted.

2. Divide the run-together sentence by using a *semicolon.*

   The spacecraft malfunctioned; the mission was aborted.

3. Divide the run-together sentence using a *comma with a coordinating word.*

   The spacecraft malfunctioned, and the mission was aborted.

4. Run-together sentences can also be corrected by combining using subordinating words, as described in Chapter 9.

   After the spacecraft malfunctioned, the mission was aborted.

Notice that a comma by itself is not sufficient to divide a run-together sentence. In fact, a sentence divided with only a comma is known as a *comma splice* and forms another kind of run-together sentence:

The party was over, we went home. ▭, ▭.

Incorrect: Comma splice

A comma splice can be corrected in four different ways:

1. The party was over. We went home. ▭. ▭.

Corrected with period

2. The party was over; we went home. ▭; ▭.

Corrected with semicolon

3. The party was over, and we went home. ▭, and ▭.

Corrected with coordinating word

4. After the party was over, we went home. ～～～, ▭.

Corrected by combining using a subordinating word

Exercise 5   *Correcting Run-Together Sentences*

1. Using each of the four methods listed below, correct the following run-together sentence:

The soap operas were an escape from the emptiness of her life my aunt watched them every day.

Corrected with period: _____

_____

Corrected with semicolon: _____

_____

Corrected with comma and coordinating word: _____

_____

Corrected by combining with a subordinating word: _____

_____

2. Using each of the four methods listed below, correct the following comma splice:

Children growing up in career military families move frequently, studies show military children are as well adjusted as other children.

Corrected with period: _____

_____

Corrected with semicolon: _____

_____

Corrected with comma and coordinating word: _____

_____

Corrected by combining with a subordinating word: _____

_____

Exercise 6   *Correcting Run-Together Sentences*

Isolate and underline the run-together sentences and comma splices in the following passage. Then rewrite the passage to correct these errors by dividing with periods or semicolons or by adding joining words with commas.

> When I came to, I couldn't feel anything in my right leg the left leg hurt terribly, however. I could see that the bone was broken it was pushing up the skin and a huge bruise was forming. My arms were OK and I could sit up I remember being thankful that I had not broken my back. I gingerly patted my head to see if everything was still in one piece it was sore and my lips were bloody, but I couldn't find any serious damage.

_____

_____

_____

_____

_____

_____

_____

_____

_____

Identifying and Correcting Nonparallel Sentences

A *parallel sentence* contains a pair or a series of items that are all expressed using the same kind of construction. Each item in the series must fit with the main part of the sentence:

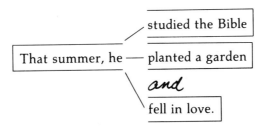

The balanced structure of a parallel sentence sets up a clear pattern that helps your reader predict and follow your meaning.

I love *apples, peaches,* and *pears.*	(All nouns)
During the triathalon, she *swam, cycled,* and *ran* for eight hours.	(All past tense verbs)
He is good at *swimming, surfing,* and *diving.*	(All -*ing* words)

In a *nonparallel sentence* the items in a pair or a series are not expressed using a parallel construction. A nonparallel sentence can be confusing to read because the structure does not fit with the reader's expectations.

Martha likes *singing, to dance,* and *reading.*	(Two -*ing* words and an infinitive)

To correct a nonparallel sentence, change the items in the series so that they are all expressed in the same form:

Martha likes *singing, dancing,* and *reading.*	(All -*ing* words)
Martha likes *to* sing, *to* dance, and *to* read.	(All infinitives)
Martha likes *songfests, dances,* and *books.*	(All nouns)

Exercise 7   *Correcting Nonparallel Sentences*

Revise the following sentences so that all items in a series are expressed in a similar form.

1. Losing the car keys made me feel angry, stupid, and fear.

    _____

    _____

2. We spent the summer playing, partying, and at the beach.

   _____

   _____

3. Fame, power, and having lots of money were Teresa's only goals.

   _____

   _____

4. She liked reading novels much more than studying for tests or to prepare her lab assignments.

   _____

   _____

5. Our quarterback had a sprained thumb, a hamstring injury, and his toe was broken.

   _____

   _____

Identifying and Correcting Verb Problems

Verbs are words that express action or a state of being. This section will help you with the following common problems involving verbs:

> Keeping verb tense consistent
> Choosing the appropriate verb tense
> Checking subject-verb agreement
> Choosing the correct irregular verb form

Keeping Verb Tense Consistent.   *Tense* simply refers to the time quality of a verb. The two most common tenses are present and past tense.
   The *present tense* shows that something is happening right now—

Jerry *looks* good, doesn't he? (right now)

—or that something usually (or habitually) happens:

A wet summer *ruins* crops. (usually)

The *past tense* shows that something happened in the past:

Jerry *looked* good yesterday.

   In writing a paper, select the tense that is most appropriate to your topic and stay with this tense unless you have a definite reason for changing it. For example, the following paragraph is written primarily in the past tense, but the final sentence uses the present tense to show that the writer *at that moment* is looking back on the past events:

We *rented* a boat and *rowed off along the shore of the lake. The boat was* broad and stable, even when we *got* up to change places. We *skimmed* along, chasing ducks and coots back into the rushes along the shoreline, until we *reached* a small cove. Then we *dropped* anchor and *began* fishing. Even today I still *remember* every part of that afternoon.

These sentences use past tense to show past action.

This sentence makes an appropriate change to present tense.

Problems arise when writing changes tense without good reason. The reader can become confused about when the actions described actually occurred:

The party began at nine o'clock, but everyone just stood around because there was no music. Finally the phone rang and the band leader ended our speculations. There is an accident: the band's van loses its brakes and runs into a tree. It proves difficult to find another vehicle large enough for the equipment. But the band finally arrived and played until two in the morning.

Notice that the writer begins in the past tense (began, stood, was, rang, ended) and then switches to the present tense (is, loses, runs, proves). Finally, the writer ends in the past tense (arrived, played).

During revision, you should check for consistent verb tense. Make sure that the main tense used in the paper is appropriate to the topic and that there is a good reason for any changes in tense.

Exercise 8   *Revising for Consistent Tense*

The following paragraph is confusing because it mixes present and past tense. Select the tense that you believe would be most appropriate and then rewrite the paragraph so that the verbs show consistent tense.

The wombat, one of several pouched mammals, lived in Australia and Tasmania. It resembles a small bear and reaches the size of a large dog. Like the kangaroo, the wombat first lived in its mother's pouch. Later, it inhabited tunnels. The wombat feeds on grass, roots, and bark. Strangely, the wombat's woodchuck-like teeth are not worn down with chewing and gnawing; they continued to grow throughout the wombat's life.

_____
_____
_____
_____
_____
_____
_____
_____

Choosing the Appropriate Verb Tense.   Present tense and past tense are two of the most common verb tenses. You will also use other tenses to show *when* a particular action occurred. Below is a review of the six major verb tenses, using the regular verb "to walk." (The form "to walk" is called the *infinitive*.)

Six Major Verb Tenses

Tense	*Example*	*Explanation*
Present	I walk	Indicates action in the present or habitual action
Past	I walked	Indicates action completed before the present
Future	I will walk	Indicates action after the present
Present perfect	I have walked	Indicates action begun in the past and still continuing
Past perfect	I had walked	Indicates action completed before another action in the past
Future perfect	I will have walked	Indicates action carried from the present to a specific time in the future

These six major tenses are formed by using the three principal parts of the verb: the *present, past,* and *past participle.* For a regular verb such as "to walk," the principal parts are constructed in the following way:

First Principal Part: Present	Second Principal Part: Past	Third Principal Part: Past Participle
Drop *to* from the infinitive	Add *-d* or *-ed* to the present	Add *-d* or *-ed* to the present
~~to~~ walk	walked	walked

The six major tenses use these three principal parts as follows:

Tense	Example	How Tense Is Formed
Present	Walk	Use first principal part
Past	Walked	Use second principal part
Future	Will walk	Use first principal part plus helping verb "will"
Present perfect	Have walked	Use third principal part plus the helping verb "have"
Past perfect	Had walked	Use third principal part plus the helping verb "had"
Future perfect	Will have walked	Use third principal part plus the helping verbs "will have"

Exercise 9   *Identifying Tenses*

In the paragraph below identify and underline each of the six major tenses of the verb "to walk." (The infinitive is marked for you.)

infinitive

In order to lose weight, I have decided <u>to walk</u> more. When I was in college, I walked everywhere I went, and consequently I never had a problem with my weight. Now I walk only when I must. My new resolution is that I will walk at least two miles a day. My plan is going well: I have walked over ten miles so far this week, and if I keep on schedule, I will have walked fourteen miles by Sunday. It was a good feeling to know that I had walked two miles this morning before my regular jelly doughnut.

Exercise 10   *Using Verb Tenses*

Form the six major tenses of the regular verb "to start." For each tense, write a sentence that shows the appropriate time period for that tense. The present tense is done for you.

1. *Present*

   start   *Every day at 6 a.m., I start my car.*

2. Past

3. Future

_____

4. Present perfect

_____

5. Past perfect

_____

6. Future perfect

_____

In addition to these six tenses, there is a progressive tense, which describes an action in *progress*. It uses a form of *be* plus the present participle (a verb ending in *-ing*):

Examples: I am walking.
              I was walking.

Checking Subject-Verb Agreement.   The form of a subject and the form of a verb in a sentence must agree. Singular subjects take singular verbs, and plural subjects take plural verbs:

Singular	*Plural*
The boy is here.	The boys are here.
I am here.	We are here.
I walk every day.	We walk every day.
He walks every day.	George and Susan walk every day.

Be alert for errors in subject-verb agreement when you revise. Below are four situations that can lead to difficulties with subject-verb agreement.

1. *Singular subjects and present tense verbs:* In the present tense, singular subjects except for *I* and *you* require an *-s* or *-es* ending on regular verbs:

Singular	*Plural*
I walk.	We walk.
You walk.	You walk.
He/she/it walk<u>s</u>.	They walk.
I teach.	We teach.
You teach.	You teach.
He/she/it teach<u>es</u>.	They teach.

This rule can be confusing because -<u>s</u> and -<u>es</u> endings form plurals when used with most nouns (one boy/two boys), but in the present tense of regular verbs, the -<u>s</u> and -<u>es</u> endings form singular verb forms to agree with singular subjects except for *I* and *you*.

This can also be confusing because some irregular verbs have special verb forms that do not use the -<u>s</u> and -<u>es</u> endings. For example, the present tense of the irregular verb "to be" is as follows:

Singular	*Plural*
I am.	We are.
You are.	You are.
He/she/it is.	They are.

Irregular verbs are discussed in greater detail on pp. 195–199.

2. *Combination subjects:* If the subject of a sentence is a *combination* of singular words, then that subject is plural and requires a plural verb:

   George drinks. (singular)

   Tom drinks. (singular)

   George and Tom drink. (plural)

   However, singular subjects joined together with the word <u>or</u> usually take a singular verb:

   George or Tom works in the store on Saturday. (singular)

3. *False subjects:* Agreement problems often arise when a writer mistakes or forgets the actual subject of a sentence and makes the verb agree instead with another word, usually one closer to the verb. For example, the following sentence presents no difficulty:

   The fragrance smells delicious.

   The singular subject (*fragrance*) takes a singular verb (*smells*). But if a plural word is added between the subject and verb, it is easy to make the mistake of changing the verb to a plural form:

   Incorrect: The fragrance of the oranges smell delicious.

   The subject is still *fragrance*, not *oranges*, so the verb should still be singular:

   Correct: The fragrance of the oranges smells delicious.

4. *Postponed subjects:* Sentences with inverted order (verb first and then subject) or sentences that begin with the word "there" can cause problems with agreement. In both cases, the postponed subject determines the form of the verb:

   Sitting in the room is one student. (singular)
   Sitting in the room are five students. (plural)

   There is one student in the room. (singular)
   There are five students in the room. (plural)

Exercise 11 *Subject-Verb Agreement*

In each sentence below, add the correct form of the indicated verb. *Use present tense.*

glow
burn
    1. Flame _____ blue at its center and _____ orange at the fringe.

curl
    2. In the valley, smoke _____ from the chimney of a lone cabin.

pass
    3. The spring and summer _____ quickly.

require
    4. A goldfish two inches long _____ at least two gallons of water.

report
    5. The police commander in each of the twenty sub-stations _____ directly to the chief.

capture
    6. That picture of the boys _____ their expressions perfectly.

wave
    7. The branches of the tall oak tree _____ in the wind.

scratch
rest
    8. The students' pencils _____ across the page and never _____, even for a minute.

scrub
dust
    9. According to the family agreement, Paul and Jean _____ the kitchen and bathroom floors, and Brenda _____ all the furniture each week.

enjoy
    10. She and I always _____ going to summer concerts.

contain
    11. A human skeleton _____ 206 bones.

filter
    12. Whales _____ tiny plants and animals from sea water with a mouth fringed with strainers called baleen.

change
    13. The color of the acids _____ quickly.

spin
dive
    14. The stunt plane _____ in the air and _____ toward the crowd.

jump
    15. Our cat always _____ at spots on the wall.

plan   16. Susan or Kay _____ to be at the meeting.

be   17. Living on the streets of this city _____
(is/are)   hundreds of young teenagers.

be   18. There _____ several safety rules that must be
(is/are)   followed in this factory.

be   19. Either your driver's license or a major credit card
(is/are)

                _____ acceptable identification for cashing a
                check.

Choosing the Correct Irregular Verb Form. As discussed on pp. 190–191, regular verbs have simple rules to determine the past and past participle. Participles are verb forms used with the helping verbs *have* or *be*.

	Helping Verb	Past Participle
I	have	walked.
I	had	walked.
You	have	walked.
She	has	walked.

For *regular* verbs, the past tense form is exactly the same as the past participle; both end in *-ed:*

Past	Past Participle
I *walked* home.	I have/had *walked* home.
It *rained* hard.	It has/had *rained* hard.
She *painted* a still life.	She has/had *painted* a still life.

Many verbs in English are *irregular.* These irregular verbs do not take -ed endings, and their past and past participle forms are usually *not* identical:

Past	Past Participle
I *forgot* the gift.	I have/had *forgotten* the gift.
He *threw* the ball.	He has/had *thrown* the ball.
She *did* her work.	She has/had *done* her work.
Snow *fell* steadily.	Snow has/had *fallen* steadily.

Because irregular verbs occur in so many forms, it is much easier to make mistakes with them than with regular verbs. For this reason, you should try to become familiar with the correct forms of irregular verbs. One way to do this is by checking the form of the verb in a dictionary. The dictionary will list the present, past, and past participle forms in that order.

present

past

past participle

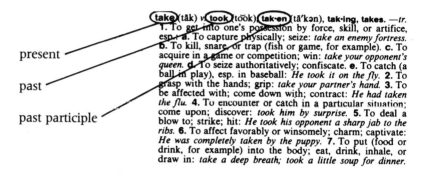

You will want to know the most common irregular verbs well enough not to have to consult a dictionary. The following list of irregular verbs probably contains many that you already know.

Present	Past	Past Participle
am (to be)	was	been
beat	beat	beaten
bend	bent	bent
bet	bet	bet
bite	bit	bitten
bleed	bled	bled
blow	blew	blown
break	broke	broken
bring	brought	brought
build	built	built
burst	burst	burst
buy	bought	bought
catch	caught	caught
choose	chose	chosen
come	came	come
creep	crept	crept
cut	cut	cut

Present	Past	Past Participle
deal	dealt	dealt
dig	dug	dug
do	did	done
draw	drew	drawn
drink	drank	drunk
drive	drove	driven
fall	fell	fallen
feed	fed	fed
feel	felt	felt
fight	fought	fought
find	found	found
fly	flew	flown
forget	forgot	forgotten
freeze	froze	frozen
get	got	got or gotten
give	gave	given
go	went	gone
grow	grew	grown
hang	hanged	hanged (executed)
hang	hung	hung (suspended)
have	had	had
hear	heard	heard
hide	hid	hid or hidden
hit	hit	hit
hold	held	held
hurt	hurt	hurt
keep	kept	kept
know	knew	known
lie	lay	lain (to recline or be situated)
lay	laid	laid (to put or place; takes object)
lead	led	led
leave	left	left
lend	lent	lent
let	let	let
lose	lost	lost

Present	Past	Past Participle
make	made	made
mean	meant	meant
meet	met	met
pay	paid	paid
put	put	put
quit	quit	quit
read	read	read
ride	rode	ridden
ring	rang	rung
rise	rose	risen
run	ran	run
say	said	said
see	saw	seen
sell	sold	sold
send	sent	sent
set	set	set
shake	shook	shaken
shine	shone	shone
shoot	shot	shot
shrink	shrank	shrunk
sing	sang	sung
sink	sank	sunk
sit	sat	sat
sleep	slept	slept
slide	slid	slid
speak	spoke	spoken
speed	sped	sped
spend	spent	spent
spread	spread	spread
stand	stood	stood
steal	stole	stolen
stick	stuck	stuck
sting	stung	stung
stink	stank	stunk

Present	Past	Past Participle
swear	swore	sworn
sweep	swept	swept
swim	swam	swum
swing	swung	swung
take	took	taken
tear	tore	torn
think	thought	thought
throw	threw	thrown
wear	wore	worn
weep	wept	wept
win	won	won
wind	wound	wound
write	wrote	written

Exercise 12   *Using the Present, Past, and Past Participle of Irregular Verbs*

In each of the following groups of sentences, use the correct present, past, or past participle form of the irregular verb.

be   1.   I _____ ready to leave now. I _____ ready several hours ago. In fact, I have _____ ready all week.

bite   2.   The dogs _____ anyone who tries to come in the yard.

Rover _____ the mail carrier last week, and now we have to pick up our mail at the post office. The statistics on the number of postal workers who have been _____ in the past year are alarming.

lie   3.   On Sundays I _____ on the sofa all morning.

Last week was worse than usual: I _____ around all day. The problem with this laziness is that after I have _____ around like this, I have no energy.

    lose   **4.**   My children constantly _____their jackets.

Last week Sammy _____a jacket and a

sweater. They have _____so many jackets that I'm having trouble finding money to buy new ones.

    ring   **5.**   The bell _____ every morning and summons the

reluctant students. Yesterday when it _____, one group in the far corner of the playground paid no attention. Not until the final tardy bell

had _____did those students slowly start toward their classes.

    lay   **6.**   Please _____the money above the cash register drawer as you make the change.

Yesterday when you _____the money in the drawer, a customer accused you of shortchanging

her. If you had _____the money above the drawer, you would not have had a problem.

Exercise 13   *Irregular Verb Forms*

In the following sentences, use the correct past or past participle form of the indicated verb.

    hang   **1.**   They _____ the rustler.

    hang   **2.**   He had _____the painting.

    lie   **3.**   The horse had _____down in the meadow.

    lay   **4.**   The chicken had _____four eggs.

    lie   **5.**   The sail _____upon the deck.

    shrink   **6.**   The pants had _____four inches.

    swear   **7.**   Tom and Huck had _____an oath.

    lead   **8.**   The guide _____them to the hut.

    rise   **9.**   They had _____early.

    lend   **10.**   Carol had _____him the money.

    hide   **11.**   They had _____the money.

    deal   **12.**   She _____the cards.

fall	13.	Mother had _____asleep.
grow	14.	Marsha _____three inches that summer.
burst	15.	The ice _____the pipes.

Identifying and Correcting Pronoun Problems

Nouns are words that name people or things. *Pronouns* are words that can refer to or replace nouns:

Noun	*Pronoun*
Marie	She, her
The man	He, him
The boys	They, their

Pronouns can also be used to show possession:

Phillip's tape deck	*His* tape deck
The girls' volleyball	*Their* volleyball
The tank's cannon	*Its* cannon

Below is a list of the most common pronouns we use:

	Singular	*Plural*
First person	I/me My, mine (possessive)	We/us Our, ours (possessive)
Second person	You Your, yours (possessive)	You Your, yours (possessive)
Third person	He/him; she/her; it His; her, hers; its (possessive)	They/them Their, theirs (possessive)

Exercise 14 *Identifying Pronouns*

In the following sentences, underline each pronoun and draw a line connecting it to the word to which it refers.

1. The berries of the festive Christmas plant mistletoe are deceiving; they are highly poisonous.
2. Venus is not difficult to identify; it is almost always the brightest star in the sky.

3. For protection, the mail carrier totes a mace cartridge in a holster hooked to his belt. He reports he has never had to use the weapon because nothing has ever attacked him.

4. The Tassles took their dog, Julie, to pet obedience school, but she was immediately suspended for her bad behavior.

5. The actor complained, "I could have been a star, but the director didn't like me and cut my part."

Correcting Pronoun Agreement Problems.   Just as verbs must agree with their subjects, pronouns must agree with the words they refer to or replace.

1. They must agree in *gender* (male or female):
Mike lost *his* wallet.
Cindy knows that *she* was wrong.

2. They must agree in *number* (singular or plural):
The *man* gathered *his* tools.
The *men* gathered *their* tools.

3. They must agree in *person* (first person refers to the *speaker;* second person to the person *spoken to;* and third person to the person or thing *spoken about*):

First person: (speaker)	*I* promise to pay *my* debts. *We* knew that *our* plane was late.
Second person: (spoken to)	Will *you* sign *your* name on this letter?
Third person: (spoken about)	*He* smiled at *his* wife. The *engine* needed an overhaul because *it* was burning oil. *They* agreed to do *their* part of the work.

Pronouns that do not agree with the words to which they refer are confusing:

Example: The city provided inadequate emergency facilities because they had budget problems.

Corrected: The city provided inadequate emergency facilities because it had budget problems.

Here, *it* (singular) agrees with *city* (singular), and the idea (that the *city* has budget problems) is clarified.

Exercise 15   *Correcting Pronoun Agreement Problems*

Revise each of the following sentences by making sure that every pronoun agrees with the word to which it refers.

1. The wall map in my den indicates which European countries share its boundaries with Communist countries.

   _____

   _____

2. John continued to talk even though I told him that you should stop.

   _____

   _____

3. A person who wants to be treated as an adult must take responsibility for their actions.

   _____

   _____

4. The avocado trees in the yard next door are beginning to drop its avocados on our side of the fence.

   _____

   _____

5. As students get used to college and learn to budget time, you find yourself getting better grades and more sleep.

   _____

   _____

Correcting Pronoun Shifts. Pronouns help to give a paper a distinct point of view. If a writer consistently uses the first person pronoun *I*, for instance, this will tend to give the writing a point of view that is more personal: "*I* felt pity for them." The second person pronoun *you* may suggest an informal, face-to-face quality: "*You* had to feel sorry for them." (In fact, this point of view is often *too* informal, unless the writer wishes to *ask* the reader a question or *tell* the reader how to do something.) Third person pronouns may be used to imply a more removed point of view: "*One* had to feel pity for them" or "*They* were pitiful."

Usually a point of view develops naturally out of the writing situation. If you were giving instructions to someone, you would probably use a "you" perspective, but if you were describing an object, you would be apt to use an "it" perspective. Most writing involves a combination of two points of view.

Problems develop only when writing shifts unnecessarily between points of view. Many of these confusing shifts involve inappropriate uses of the second person (*you*):

Last Saturday, *I* attended a rally against nuclear weapons at a naval station near *my* house. For the most part, the people at the rally were peaceful and courteous. *They* were careful not to block traffic, and *they* didn't try to enter the base itself. *I* was glad about this, because *you* never want to be arrested. The demonstrators wanted the navy to move any nuclear weapons to a more remote base, but the navy press officer would not even confirm or deny that weapons were kept on the base. *You* had to expect that, since *it* was what *he* had always said before.

Note that the first person (*I, my*) and third person (*they, it*) points of view are appropriate to the writing situation: one person describing the actions of others. The two uses of *you* (second person) seem out of place, however, because they incorrectly imply that *you*, the reader, were somehow there at the naval base. The sentences containing *you* might be revised as follows:

Original	*Revision*
I was glad about this, because *you* never want to be arrested.	I was glad about this, because *I* didn't want to be arrested.
You had to expect that, since it was what he had always said before.	*One* had to expect that, since it was what he had always said before.

To avoid unnecessary shifts of perspective, choose a point of view that is appropriate to the writing situation and stick with it. During revision, correct any pronoun shifts that disrupt your paper's point of view.

Exercise 16   *Correcting Pronoun Shifts*

Revise the following passage so that it is written in the first person (*I, we*):

When I think back to my childhood, I realize that my parents kept my brother and me in line with the help of several mythological characters. For instance, Santa wasn't always the jolly, rotund figure of good cheer that children expect. My parents let you know that your bad behavior might displease Santa. You could get coal in your stocking. Worse yet, we might get only the "little things" on our lists. The boogey man also kept us in line. He helped my parents get us home before dark, for you could be snatched off the sidewalk if you wandered home after the sun had set. Even the tooth fairy had her nasty side: She refused to take a tooth with a cavity in it. We brushed regularly, knowing that if you didn't, a rotten tooth would still be under the pillow in the morning.

_____

_____

_____

_____

_____

_____

_____

_____

_____

_____

_____

_____

_____

_____

_____

_____

PUNCTUATION SKILLS _____

The pauses, gestures, facial expressions, whispers, and shouts you use to help get your message across when you talk can't help you when you write. You won't be there to interpret your writing for the reader. But you do have a tool to help get across the spirit and meaning of what you want to say: punctuation.

Generally, punctuation follows established rules, which we review below. However, even English teachers sometimes disagree as to whether or not a comma belongs in a particular sentence or whether a colon or a dash is more effective in another sentence. Furthermore, the meaning of the sentence can determine the punctuation. For example, look at these two sets of sentences:

The Democrats say the Republicans will lose the next election.
The Democrats, say the Republicans, will lose the next election.

Calling my friends names, I ran desperately after them.
Calling my friends' names, I ran desperately after them.

In the first set, who is going to lose? In the second set, will your friends be insulted? The sentences in each set have different meanings. The writer must punctuate according to his or her intention or meaning.

You are responsible for deciding what punctuation works best in any writing you do. The following guidelines will help you.

1. Don't worry about punctuation early in the writing process.
2. When you are ready to edit for punctuation, read your writing aloud. As you do, your "sentence sense," a feel for the ways sentences are structured in English, will help you find where sentences naturally end. Check that the sentences have end punctuation—periods or question marks. The places where you find yourself pausing in the middle of a sentence probably need commas.
3. Keep your readers in mind when you check your punctuation. Remember that each mark of punctuation gives them a specific message and helps guide them through your writing.
4. Don't use a mark of punctuation unless you can justify it. Some papers look as if the writer stood over the final draft and sprinkled commas everywhere. Reading such a paper is like driving with someone who slams on the brakes every fifty feet.
5. Other punctuation marks—semicolon, dash, underlining, even an occasional exclamation mark—are effective when used sparingly, but when they are overused they are irritating to a reader.

Commas

The comma has four main uses:

1. To join two sentences, before a coordinating word
2. To set off introductory material in a sentence
3. To set off added material that interrupts the flow of a sentence
4. To separate items in a series

Comma Before a Coordinating Word.   Use a comma before a joining word, a coordinating conjunction that joins two independent sentences.

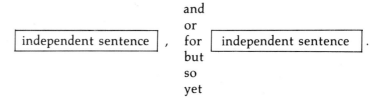

Examples:

A heavy gray sky seemed to press down on us, and we knew it would bring rain.

Our only comfort came in knowing we could remain dry and warm, for we had brought our tent.

Make sure you are joining together two complete sentences. Each sentence must have a subject and a verb. As a check, underline the subject with one line and the verb with two lines.

Use comma: He <u>staggered</u> out of the bar, and the <u>door</u> <u>slammed</u> behind him.

No comma: He <u>staggered</u> out and <u>collapsed</u> on the sidewalk.

The second sentence has two verbs. If you put a comma after *out,* the reader will expect a complete sentence to follow *and.* However, some writers don't use the comma when the sentences are very short: The whistle blew and play stopped.

Exercise 17 *Using a Comma Before a Joining Word*

Each of the following examples consists of two independent sentences connected with a joining word. Supply the necessary comma in each example.

1. Children's toys are now the product of painstaking research and development costs for one toy can run into the millions of dollars.
2. The cheetah can run an amazing seventy miles per hour but it can maintain this speed only for short distances.
3. The baby may be coming down with another respiratory infection or he may have an allergy that has not been identified.

Write three sentences of your own in this pattern (two independent sentences with a comma before a joining word).

1. _____

_____

2. _____

_____

3. _____

_____

Comma to Set Off Introductory Material. Use a comma to set off an introductory word or word group.

introductory word or word group, | main part of sentence |

Examples:

Next, we cleaned the interior of the car.

During the night, a light snow fell.

Although I had studied diligently, I did poorly on the test.

Because I felt sick, I went to the student health service.

In the third and fourth examples, *although* and *because* introduce dependent word groups that can't stand alone as sentences. (If you went up to someone and said, "Because I felt sick," the other person would wait expectantly for the rest of the thought.) The comma after *Because I felt sick* tells readers that they have come to the end of the dependent word group and are starting the main part of the sentence. If the sentence were turned around and written, *I went to the student health service because I felt sick,* you would need no comma.

To test the necessity of a comma after an introductory word group, try reading this sentence:

After throwing out his roommate John started cleaning the messy apartment.

Most readers stumble, thinking at first that John is the roommate's name. In the correctly punctuated example below, the confusion is cleared up.

After throwing out his roommate, John started cleaning the messy apartment.

Note: Sentences with introductory dependent word groups are common in well-written English. For more examples of such sentences and a list of subordinate conjunctions like *although* and *because* that start these word groups, see p. 145 in Chapter 9.

Exercise 18   *Using a Comma to Set Off an Introductory Word or Word Group*

Each of the following examples has an introductory word or word group that should be set off with a comma. Supply the necessary comma.

1. After the boss carefully explained the new procedures we were less confused.
2. In the winter of 1982–83 heavy rains caused the river to flood.
3. Yes I agree with your decision.

Write three sentences of your own in this pattern (an introductory word or word group set off with a comma). Begin one sentence with the word *after, although,* or *because.*

1. _____

   _____

2. _____

_____

3. _____

_____

Comma to Set Off Added Material.   Use commas to set off words or word groups added to a sentence in order to explain, describe, or clarify, if those words or word groups interrupt the flow of a sentence.

| main sentence | , | interrupter | , | continuation of main sentence |

Examples:

This drug, however, has fewer side effects.

Bob, who grew up in Idaho, finds California a strange place to live.

Dr. Nikelson, a local pediatrician, spoke to the parents' groups about new techniques for treating hyperactive children.

Commas are not used to set off interrupting words or word groups that *cannot be left out* because they are essential to the meaning of the sentence.

The patient who took vitamins got better; the patient who took aspirin did not.

Here the information introduced by *who* is essential in distinguishing between the patients. Compare: "The patient, who took vitamins, lived mainly on junk food."

When you have a direct quotation, set off with commas words such as *I said*, and *he asked.* These interrupting words may come anywhere in the sentence.

"A little money," the developer commented, "will make this tropical lagoon a lucrative tourist resort."

The developer commented, "A little money will make this tropical lagoon a lucrative tourist resort."

If an idea that is clearly an afterthought is added at the end of a sentence, you may decide to set it off with a comma.

I hung up in despair, knowing he would never call again.

Reading your writing aloud will help you decide if you need to set off added material. Generally, you put commas in the places where you naturally pause.

Exercise 19   *Using Commas to Set Off Words or Word Groups That Interrupt the Flow of a Sentence*

Each of the following sentences contains words or word groups that interrupt the flow of the sentence and are not essential to the meaning of the sentence. Supply the necessary commas.

1. The facts therefore do not support your conclusions.
2. My brother-in-law who is a health fanatic gets more colds than anyone I know.
3. "The Super Bowl" the sociologist commented "has become an annual national ritual for millions of Americans."
4. Jim Dorman the new shop steward will file a grievance.
5. We pulled into our driveway happy to be home.

Write three or four sentences of your own in this pattern (added words or word groups set off with commas).

1. _____

   _____

2. _____

   _____

3. _____

   _____

Comma to Separate Items in a Series.   Use commas to separate words and word groups used in a series.

_____, _____, and _____

Examples:

For dinner we had salad, steak, and potatoes.
The dealer had models available in black, white, and blue.

Some writers leave out the comma before *and* in the sentence above. However, the sentence is clearer with that comma. Otherwise, a reader may think two models (one black, one white and blue) are available.

Example:

Last summer, Jack hiked in the mountains, fished the lakes, and rafted down the river near his camp.

Sometimes the word groups could stand alone as separate sentences, but they are not run-on sentences when they are structured as a series.

Example:

I read all the required material, I attended every class, and I turned in all my written work.

Use a comma between two descriptive words that both modify the same word or word group. A test to check whether you need a comma is that the comma could be replaced by the word *and*.

Examples:

The calloused, scarred hands were mute testimony to years of hard work.
The badly scarred hands were mute testimony to years of hard work.

In the first sentence, you could say, "The calloused and scarred hands . . ." But the second sentence needs no comma because *badly* and *scarred hands* doesn't sound right; the word *badly* modi⌐es the word *scarred*, not the word *hands*.

Exercise 20 *Using Commas to Separate Items in a Series*

Each of the following examples has words or word groups used in a series. Supply the necessary commas.

1. The sting of a bee hornet or wasp can cause a severe reaction in some people.
2. The high desert is a harsh arid environment.
3. Small cuts should be washed for several minutes with fresh water covered with a bandage and watched for signs of infection.
4. Soon the empty parking lot will be jammed every seat in the stadium will be filled and the first game of the World Series will begin.

Write three sentences of your own in this pattern (word or word groups used in a series).

1. _____

_____

2. _____

_____

3. _____

_____

Semicolons

The semicolon is a simple and effective way of linking two sentences together. It can add style and variety to your writing and is especially useful when the relationship between two ideas is close but difficult to express in words.

independent sentence   independent sentence

[_____] ;   [_____] .

You won't get into trouble with semicolons if you remember to use them only where you could also use a period.

Example:

I walked away without saying a word. I regret that moment.

or

I walked away without saying a word; I regret that moment.

The semicolon is also useful when you are setting up contrasting ideas.

Example:

The mother with a career is criticized for neglecting her child; the mother who stays home is criticized for smothering her child.

Semicolons can also be used with transitional words and phrases such as the following:

also	likewise	thus	instead
anyway	meanwhile	furthermore	in fact
besides	moreover	as a result	in other words
consequently	nevertheless	at any rate	in the second place
finally	next	at the same time	on the other hand
however	otherwise	even so	in addition
indeed	then	therefore	for example

independent sentence with

independent sentence   *transitional word or phrase*

    ☐ ; ☐ .

Examples:

Geologists believe oil exists in Antarctica. However, ecologists worry about the effect of oil drilling on that continent's fragile environment.

or

Geologists believe oil exists in Antarctica; however, ecologists worry about the effect of oil drilling on that continent's fragile environment.

or

Geologists believe oil exists in Antarctica; ecologists, however, worry about the effect of oil drilling on that continent's fragile environment.

(Since *however* is part of the second sentence, you can move it around to change the emphasis.)

There is one exception to the rule that semicolons replace periods. They can help untangle sentences in which many commas in a long series cause confusion. Consider the following sentence:

The following door prizes and their donors should be listed on the program: a ten-speed bike, Bayside Cycle Shop, gift certificate, Smith's Food Market, portable black and white television, Ron's Appliance Center, drip coffeepot, Glasgow's Housewares, and dinner for two, Mom's Cafe.

Semicolons can make this list much easier to read:

The following door prizes and their donors should be listed on the program: a ten-speed bike, Bayside Cycle Shop; gift certificate, Smith's Food Market; portable black and white television, Ron's Appliance Center; drip coffeepot, Glasgow's Housewares; and dinner for two, Mom's Cafe.

Exercise 21   *Using Semicolons*

Each of the following examples has two independent sentences. Use a semicolon to link them.

1. Throughout the world, the amount of land covered with forests is decreasing. Lumber production, paper making, and firewood gathering are some of the causes of this deforestation.

2. An insufficient supply of vitamin A can cause respiratory, skin, or eye problems. However, an excessive supply of the vitamin also causes problems.

3. I received a high score on the written exam and the oral interview. I believe, therefore, that I have a good chance of getting a job with the fire department.

4. The student who failed the psychology course turned in only two of the four required assignments. Furthermore, she did not show up for the final examination.

Write four examples of your own in this pattern (independent sentences linked with a semicolon). In at least two of your examples, use transitional words from the above list. Remember that the two sentences in each example should have a close relationship.

1. _____

_____

2. _____

_____

3. _____

_____

Colons

The colon is used after a complete sentence to introduce a word, a list, another sentence, or a long quotation. It draws your reader's attention to the specifics you offer in support of some point.

| complete sentence | : _____ .

1. Introducing a word:
   Your behavior can be summed up in one word: disgraceful.

2. Introducing a list:
   The following movies are among Hollywood's worst: *Cat Women of the Moon, Attack of the Killer Tomatoes, The Horror of Party Beach,* and *Invasion of the Saucer Men.*

3. Introducing an explanatory sentence:
   He was a difficult child: whenever he didn't get his way, he threw a screaming tantrum.

4. Introducing a long quotation:
   In his book, *The Right Stuff,* Tom Wolfe comments on the popularity of the first seven astronauts: "By the next morning the seven Mer-

cury astronauts were national heroes. It happened just like that. Even though so far they had done nothing more than show up for a press conference, they were known as the seven bravest men in America." (pp. 99–100)

A colon also helps eliminate unnecessary words. The italicized words in the first example below are replaced by a colon in the second example.

> *Original:* Oil drilling in the Arctic could affect many species. *Some of these species are* seabirds, seals, polar bears, white foxes, whales, musk-oxen, and caribou.
>
> *Revision:* Oil drilling in the Arctic could affect many species: seabirds, seals, polar bears, white foxes, whales, musk-oxen, and caribou.

Remember that a colon follows a complete sentence. You would *not* put a colon after *such as* in the following example:

> *A good breakfast includes nutritious foods such as fruit, whole wheat cereal, and milk.*

Exercise 22   *Using Colons*

Each of the following examples has a complete sentence that introduces a word, a list, another sentence or a quotation. Supply the appropriate colon in each example.

1. A number of steps could be taken to reduce fatalities from all-terrain vehicles require that all ATV operators pass a safety course, make wearing of helmets by operators and passengers mandatory, and regulate where the vehicles may be driven.

2. The following students need to schedule a conference John Phillips, Christine Brown, and Lewis Garcia.

3. In his 1934 message to Congress, President Roosevelt made the following statement about the arms race "This grave menace to the peace of the world is due in no small measure to the uncontrolled activities of the manufacturers and merchants of engines of destruction, and it must be met by the concerted action of the peoples of all nations."

Write three examples of your own, using a colon.

1. _____

_____

2. _____

   _____

3. _____

   _____

Dashes

The dash—two hyphens on the typewriter—is a useful and versatile mark of punctuation. The dash can take the place of the comma, semi-colon, or period when you want to emphasize something.

Remember, though, that the dash is informal and dramatic and should be used sparingly, especially in formal writing.

Examples:

Dashes are used instead of commas to set off—and emphasize— material added to a sentence.

She asked—in fact, she demanded—that he get out of her life.

She asked him to get out of her life—immediately.

The new rules—which I was against at first—have improved the discipline at the junior high school.

He was fired for missing too much work—he had called in sick every Monday for a month.

Parentheses

Parentheses ( ) set off extra material that you want to slip into a sentence. They have the opposite effect of a dash: a dash emphasizes; parentheses play down. Use parentheses for material that is *not* essential to the meaning of a sentence.

Parentheses can set off dates, page references, word groups, and complete sentences.

Examples:

Nicholos Copernicus (1473–1543) first advanced the theory that the sun, not the earth, is the center of our solar system.

Like Galileo (see page 469), Copernicus was trained in medicine but was primarily interested in mathematics and astronomy.

The meeting (originally scheduled for 10 A.M.) began at 2 P.M.

His grandmother is still athletic. (I believe she was once a dancer.)

Note that when a complete sentence is inside parentheses, the period also goes inside, as in the last example above.

Parentheses are especially useful when you need to explain or define a term your reader may not know.

Example:

The computer program is stored on a floppy disk (a thin, flexible 5¼-inch plastic diskette).

Exercise 23   *Using Dashes and Parentheses*

The following examples contain extra material that should be set off with either dashes or parentheses. Punctuate the examples appropriately, referring to the above sections on dashes and parentheses if you need help. Remember that dashes emphasize and parentheses play down.

1. There is one thing you must remember to pack for the camping trip your sleeping bag.
2. That book on computer programming which I haven't had time to look at yet is supposed to be the most helpful guide available.
3. John F. Kennedy 1917–1963 was the youngest person ever elected president of the United States.
4. The diner with its red Naugahyde booths, Formica-topped tables, and long counter looked like something right out of the fifties.

Write four examples of your own, two using dashes and two using parentheses.

1. _____

   _____

2. _____

   _____

3. _____

   _____

4. _____

   _____

Hyphens

The hyphen (-) helps your reader in several ways:

1. A hyphen connects words that work together as a single unit.

Examples:

go-between, old-timer, make-up, ex-husband, self-confidence

Check your dictionary: sometimes these words are hyphenated; sometimes they are acceptable as one word or two separate words.

2. The hyphen is used with two or more words working together as a descriptive unit before a noun.

Examples:

mind-boggling experience, fast-moving storm, half-full stadium, twentieth-century literature, two-thirds majority, two-by-four post, twenty-five-year-old woman, bluish-green eyes

Notice that each word in the unit is necessary. The eyes are not green and are not blue; they are bluish-green.

3. Hyphenate compound numbers between twenty-one and ninety-nine.

4. Use a hyphen to divide a word at the end of a line. Consult your dictionary to make certain you divide the word between two syllables.

5. Use a hyphen when necessary to clarify your writing.

I re-covered that chair.

This sentence means that you put new material on it, not that you recovered a stolen chair.

If you're not convinced hyphens can clarify writing, try to read the following sentence:

The thirty nine year old carpenter bought fifty two two by four boards.

A reader giving the above sentence a quick look could be confused. Hyphens clarify the sentence:

The thirty-nine-year-old carpenter bought fifty-two two-by-four boards.

Exercise 24   Using Hyphens

The following paragraph needs seventeen hyphens. Supply them. The paragraph will be easier to read when the hyphens have been added.

My twenty two year old husband, twenty seven year old brother in law, and I decided to join a self help group. Being in the group was a mind boggling experience. We met for a two hour session twice a week. Two thirds of the members were very negative; in fact they seemed almost anti American. One blue eyed lady with a know it all look was especially critical of everything. This self help group was a disaster: now my husband is my ex husband.

Quotation Marks

Use quotation marks to set off the exact words of a speaker.

Examples:

"Let me see your license," the police officer said.

"Feeding the bears," the ranger warned, "is forbidden. They may develop a taste for human food and keep coming back looking for handouts even after they are moved to remote areas of the park. Sometimes such bears must be destroyed."

Note that the *exact words* of the police officer and of the ranger are set off with quotation marks. Interrupting words such as *the ranger warned* are set off with commas (see Commas, pp. 206–211). The second part of the ranger's speech has two sentences with no interrupting words. In such a case, put quotation marks at the beginning and end of the quoted material, not around each sentence.

Use quotation marks to set off another writer's exact words that you quote to support your own point, as in the following example:

If we are ever to reduce our high crime rate, we must understand why crime occurs. According to Ramsey Clark, a former Attorney General of the United States, "The motives of most crimes are economic. Seven of eight known serious crimes involve property." (*Crime in America*, p. 24)

You may decide to use more of another writer's words. Long quotations (more than four typewritten lines) are set off by indenting the whole quotation and do not need quotation marks. Indenting long quotations allows your reader to keep straight which are your words and which are someone else's.

When we think of crime, we tend to think of murder, assault, robbery, and burglary. We forget that we are also the victims of white-collar crime:

Illicit gains from white-collar crime far exceed those of all other crime combined. Crime as practiced among the poor is more dangerous and less profitable. One corporate price-fixing conspiracy criminally converted more money each year it continued than all of the hundreds of thousands of burglaries, larcenies, or thefts in the entire nation during those same years. Reported bank embezzlements, deposits diverted by bank employees, cost ten times more than bank robberies each year. (Ramsey Clark, *Crime in America*, p. 23)

Periods and commas always go inside quotation marks.

Examples:

"Let me see your license," the police officer said.

The police officer said, "Let me see your license."

Colons and semicolons go outside quotation marks.

Example:

The police officer said, "Let me see your license"; I started to shake.

Question marks go inside if just the quotation is a question and outside if the whole sentence is a question.

Examples:

"Do you have a license?" the police officer said.
Did the police officer say, "Let me see your license"?

Indirect quotations—when you put someone else's words into your own words—do not need quotation marks. Indirect quotations often follow the word *that.* Compare this direct quotation with the indirect quotation:

Direct quotation: "Let me see your license," the police officer said.
Indirect quotation: The police officer told me that he wanted to see my license.

Remember that when you use another writer's ideas in a paper—even if you put those ideas into your own words—you must give credit to that writer by giving your source. Of course, if you do put the ideas in your own words, do not use quotation marks.

Setting Off Titles

Use *quotation marks* to set off titles of short works or parts of works: short stories, songs, articles in magazines, chapters in books.

Use *underlining* to set off titles of long works or separate publications: books, magazines, newspapers, albums, movies, television programs. In published material, titles of long works or separate publications are set in italic type like this: *The Red Badge of Courage.*

Using quotation marks and underlining for titles helps your reader sort through a sentence with several titles.

Examples:

"India Struggles to Save Her Wildlife" in National Geographic describes that country's efforts to save the tiger from extinction.

Both the album The Stranger and one of the cuts from it, "Just the Way You Are," were big sellers for Billy Joel.

Note: Do not set off the titles of your own papers with quotation marks or underlining.

Exercise 25   *Using Quotation Marks and Italics or Underlining*

The following passage needs quotation marks and underlining. Remember that quotation marks are used for two purposes: (1) to set off a quotation or the exact words of a speaker and (2) to set off titles of short works or parts of works. Underlining sets off titles of long works or separate publications. If you need help, refer to the sections above on quotation marks and setting off titles.

In my communications class, I was assigned a speech on the topic of leisure activity. I asked my dad for advice. He told me that I should start with a quote from someone famous: I looked at him and said, Thanks, but where do I look for such a quote?

He replied, Try the book Bartlett's Familiar Quotations.

In that book, I found the perfect quote, a line from Mark Twain's The Adventures of Tom Sawyer: Work consists of whatever a body is obliged to do, and play consists of whatever a body is not obliged to do. Next I read an article called New Uses for Leisure Time in our local newspaper, The Daily Chronicle. I found another article entitled The Psychological Benefits of Exercise in the magazine Psychology Today. With the information from these articles and my own ideas, I had enough material for my speech.

Forming Contractions with Apostrophes

Contractions—two words combined into one—are common in speech and writing. Some writers believe, however, that contractions should not be used in research papers and formal reports.

When you write a contraction, insert an apostrophe to show where letters have been left out.

Example:
Don't (formed from *do not;* the second *o* is left out)

Common Contractions

I'd (I had or I would)	We'll (we will)
I'll (I will)	We're (we are)
I'm (I am)	You'll (you will)
I've (I have)	You're (you are)
He'd (he would or he had)	You've (you have)
He'll (he will)	They're (they are)
She'd (she would or she had)	They've (they have)
It's (it is or it has)	There's (there is)
Who's (who is)	
Aren't (are not)	Hasn't (has not)
Couldn't (could not)	Isn't (is not)
Didn't (did not)	Weren't (were not)

Common Contractions

Doesn't (does not)   Won't (will not—notice spelling
                                                    of contraction)

'55 Chevy (1955 Chevy)   o'clock (of the clock)

Showing Possession

You can show possession or ownership in three ways:

1. With possessive pronouns such as *my, mine, his, hers, its, yours, our, ours, their, theirs,* and *whose*

   Examples:
   The security officer lets *his* dog bark all night.
   Clint wrecked *his* pickup truck.
   The company sent dividend checks to *its* stockholders.

2. With words such as *owned, belongs,* or *of*

   Examples:
   The security officer *owns* the dog that barks all night.
   The wrecked pickup truck *belongs* to Clint.
   The stockholders *of* the company received dividend checks.

3. With an apostrophe (')

   Examples:
   The security officer's dog barks all night.
   Clint's pickup truck is wrecked.
   The company's stockholders received dividend checks.

If you have used an apostrophe to show possession, check whether you have used it correctly:

1. Decide whether you need a singular or plural word. Some singular forms end in *s* (*waitress*) and some plural forms do not end in *s* (*children*). Check your dictionary if you are not sure of the plural form.

2. Make sure you need a possessive form. (Could you rewrite the sentence with *of, own,* or *belong?*)

3. If your word does not end in *s,* add an *'s.* If your word ends in *s,* add only an apostrophe.

Usually you show possession in singular words by adding an *'s* (*one boy's hat*) and in plural words just add an apostrophe (*all the boys' hats*). Singular words that end in *s* (*waitress*) and plural words that do not end in *s* (*children*) are exceptions to this rule (*the waitress' paycheck, the children's toys*).

However, note: some style manuals prefer the use of *'s* for all singular possessives, even those which already end in *s* (*the waitress's paycheck, Chris's truck*).

Exercise 26 *Using Apostrophes*

Decide whether or not you need to add an apostrophe to each underlined word in the following sentences.

1. If the word is a contraction, insert an apostrophe where letters have been left out. (See the section above on contractions.)
2. If the word shows possession, decide if you need an apostrophe. (See the section above on possession.)

Example:
It's not considered wise to insult your Dad's boss.

1. Theres a campaign meeting tonight, but Im not sure whose turn it is to supply refreshments.
2. That man looks after his dog better than he does his children. The childrens faces are dirty, and one little boys jacket isnt warm enough for this weather. The faces of the two little girls have a pinched, thin look. Its not a good situation.
3. Isnt that Joes truck parked next to the neighbors house?
4. The waitress uniform wasnt very clean. The food didnt come for over an hour. That restaurant certainly has its problems.
5. Johns career plans are still vague.

Capitals

The following rules will help you decide whether or not a word should be capitalized. Do not capitalize a word unless you have a reason for doing so. Capital letters help your reader pick out the proper names and titles in your writing. Capitals used unnecessarily will confuse your reader. If you don't know whether to capitalize a word, check your dictionary.

1. Capitalize the first word of every sentence and the first word of directly quoted speech. Always capitalize the word *I*.

Examples:

With good binoculars, the amateur astronomer can see the rings of Saturn.

Turning to my mother, *I* said, "When will dinner be ready?"

2. Capitalize proper names of specific people, places, products, languages, courses, religions, political organizations, and racial groups.

Capitals	*No Capitals*
Joe Smith	
President Lincoln	the president of our club
Sister Mary Margaret, a nun	my younger sister
Colorado	the state he lives in
the Grand Canyon	the river flowed through the canyon
the Hudson River	
New Zealand	
the East	drive east two miles
the Midwest	
Canadian geese	birch trees
Crest toothpaste	
English, Spanish, French	a foreign language
Chemistry IA	a course in chemistry
Christianity	
Moslem	
the Democrats	a democratic system
Amnesty International	
United Nations	
Boy Scouts of America	
Americana	
Irish	

3. Capitalize names of days of the week, months, holidays, and historical events.

Capitals	*No Capitals*
Sunday	tomorrow
April	spring vacation
Christmas	
Chanukah	
World War II	the two world wars
the Depression	the twentieth century

4. Capitalize the first word and last word and all main words in titles.

Examples:
The Red Badge of Courage

All the President's Men

How to Win Friends and Influence People

"The Burger that Conquered the Country"

"What the Desert Means to Me"

5. Capitalize most abbreviations.

Examples:

Mr. Brown, Mrs. Brown, Ms. Brown, Dr. Brown

J. R. Smith, M.D.

ABC, NBC, CBS, FBI, NASA (These are familiar abbreviations; if you use an unfamiliar abbreviation, be sure to write out the full name the first time you refer to it.)

10:35 A.M. (a.m. is also acceptable)

Numbers

1. Write out numbers that take only one or two words.

Examples:

Forty dollars

Twenty-one students

Ten o'clock

The twentieth century

2. Use numerals for numbers that take more than two words.

Examples:

343 students

$29.43

2.5 percent

Be consistent. If you write some numbers in numerals, then use numerals for all the numbers in that piece of writing.

3. Use numerals for dates, times, addresses, and references to page numbers.

Examples:

April 9, 1982

The War of 1812

The 1980's (or 1980s)

10:45 A.M. (or a.m.)

1600 East 22nd Street, New York, NY 10010

Chapter 5, p. 46

TROUBLESOME WORDS

The following word pairs (or triplets) often cause confusion and spelling problems for writers. Read the list and familiarize yourself with these words so that when you use one of them you'll remember to check it here.

a lot

a lot: a large number or amount (noun)

Never write as *alot*. Write "I have *a lot* of friends." If possible, use a more precise term.

accept/except

accept: to take, receive (verb)

I *accept* your apology.

except: but (preposition)

Everyone left the party *except* Harry.

advice/advise

advice: opinion, counsel (noun)

When I want your *advice*. I'll ask for it!

advise: to offer advice (verb)

My parents *advised* me to apply to several colleges.

affect/effect

affect: to influence (verb)

Staying out all night may *affect* my performance on the test.

effect: result (noun)

We don't know the long-term *effect* of that drug.

bring about, execute (verb)

Joan will *effect* great changes in the day-care program.

aisle/I'll/isle

aisle: a passageway

They marched down the *aisle*.

I'll: contraction of *I will*

I'll call you later today.

isle: a small island

Let's sail to some deserted *isle*.

all ready/already

all ready: prepared, available

We were *all ready* to go.

already: before, previously (always *one* word)

I *already* took my vitamins.

all right

all right: satisfactory, correct; yes; uninjured (adverb)

Do not write as *alright*. "Are you *all right*?" is the correct form.

all together/altogether

all together: in a group

Their families were *all together* at the funeral.

altogether: entirely, completely

Altogether, 55 percent of the eligible voters turned out.

among/between

among: in the midst of

You are *among* friends.

between: in the space separating two objects

I'm *between* a rock and a hard place.

amount/number
few/less

amount/number;
few/less: all indicate quantity

Amount and *less* take a singular (or collective) noun: "I have *less* money today." "What is the *amount* of sugar you want?" *Number* and *few,* on the other hand, take plural (and countable) nouns: "He has a *number* of jobs." "I only have a *few* dollars."

an/and

an: a

I ate *an* apple.

and: together, along with

I love apples *and* peaches.

are/hour/our

are: present tense of *be* (verb)

Are you coming or not?

hour: time of day (noun)

It's ten minutes past the *hour.*

our: possessive form of *we* (pronoun)

It's *our* decision.

ate/eight

ate: past tense of *eat* (verb)

I *ate* dinner early.

eight: number (noun)

There were *eight* courses.

bare/bear

bare: naked, undisguised (adjective)

That baby was completely *bare.*

bear: to carry, support (verb)

Learn to grin and *bear* it!

large, omnivorous animal (noun)

A black *bear* ran through our camp.

beside/besides

beside: next to, at the side of (preposition)

Sit down *beside* me here.

besides: in addition, also (adverb)

Besides, we already know what Mom will say.

board/bored

board: a flat piece of wood (noun)

The fence was made of long pine *boards.*

bored: past tense of *bore* (verb)

The dull, dry lecturer *bored* the audience.

brake/break

brake: to slow down or stop (verb)

Try to brake smoothly.

something that slows or stops action (noun)

Tom slammed on the *brakes.*

break: to crack, split (verb)

He tried to *break* my spirit.

the act of breaking (noun)

There was a *break* in the action.

buy/by

buy: to purchase (verb)

I want to *buy* a new car.

by: next to, close to (preposition)

There was a skunk *by* the road.

capital/capitol

capital: the seat of government; wealth; upper-case letter

Santa Fe is the *capital* of New Mexico.

Businesses without adequate *capital* often fail.

Sentences should start with *capital* letters.

capitol: the building in which a legislative assembly sits

We went to our state *capitol* in high school.

choose/chose

choose: to select, pick

You can *choose* only one.

chose: past tense of *choose*

I *chose* the dress yesterday.

cite/sight/site

cite: to quote, mention (verb)

He *cited* many works in his paper.

sight: the act of seeing, ability to see (noun)

They restored her *sight* in a five-hour operation.

site: the place where something is located (noun)

The city council finally found a *site* for the new stadium.

close/clothes/cloths

close: near in time or space (adjective)

It was a *close* call.

to shut (verb)

Close the door when you leave.

clothes: articles of wear (noun)	He didn't have all his *clothes* on.
cloths: pieces of fabric (noun)	Bright *cloths* covered the tables.

coarse/course

coarse: rough, inferior (adjective)	Polly uses very *coarse* language.
course: direction, route; time; series of studies (noun)	The boats followed the *course* carefully.

conscience/conscious

conscience: moral, ethical values (noun)	You've got to follow your *conscience* in this matter.
conscious: awake, aware (adjective)	He was *conscious* of a strange feeling in the old house.

could hardly

hardly: barely, just (adverb)	Do not write "I couldn't hardly see." Write "I could *hardly* see."

council/counsel

council: an adminstrative body	Jeff is president of the student *council.*
counsel: advise (verb)	Pastor Baker *counsels* couples before they get married.
advice (noun)	Couples find his *counsel* valuable.

councilor/counselor

councilor: member of a council	That *councilor* was recalled in the last election.
counselor: a person who gives counsel or advice	My guidance *counselor* got me into college.

desert/dessert

desert: a dry, barren region (noun)	The *desert* was hot and treeless.
to forsake, leave (verb)	He *deserted* his outfit.
dessert: last course of a meal (noun)	We had plum cake for *dessert.*

effect: see affect

except: see accept

everyday/every day

everyday: common, routine	That's an *everyday* worry to me.
every day: one day after another	He wore his new suit *every day* for a week.

fair/fare

fair: lovely; light; just (adjective)

The weather was *fair* and clear.

a specific gathering (noun)

We're going to the county *fair*.

fare: to get along (verb)

How did you *fare* on the test?

transportation charge (noun)

What's the *fare* to Chester?

for/fore/four

for: preposition used to indicate object, aim, or purpose

He left *for* town about an hour ago.

fore: located at or toward the front

Sally has really come to the *fore*.

four: number

Frank had *four* beers before lunch.

formally/formerly

formally: done properly or regularly

He was dressed quite *formally* for such an occasion.

formerly: once, at a former time

He was *formerly* president of the Chamber of Commerce.

forth/fourth

forth: forward in time, place, or order

Penny rushed *forth* without thinking.

fourth: number

He finally passed the bar exam the *fourth* time he took it.

have/of

have: auxiliary (helping) verb

Do not use "of" in place of "have." Write "I could *have* killed him," instead of "I could *of* killed him."

heal/heel/he'll

heal: to cure, repair (verb)

Her scar *healed* nicely.

heel: part of the foot or shoe (noun)

Bill's shoes definitely need new *heels*.

he'll: contraction of *he will*

He'll come back tomorrow.

hear/here

hear: to listen, perceive (verb)

Do you *hear* what I'm saying?

here: at, in this place (adverb)

Don't stop *here*.

hole/whole

hole: opening, cavity (noun)

There's a *hole* in the roof.

whole: complete, healthy (adjective)

They can't believe they ate the *whole* thing.

all parts of a thing (noun)

We should consider the grades as a *whole*.

idea/ideal

idea: thought, opinion (noun)

I have an *idea* Sally will be back.

ideal: goal; standard; principle (noun)

Justice was her *ideal*.

perfect; imaginary (adjective)

His timing was *ideal*.

imply/infer

imply: to state indirectly

By his statement, the judge *implied* we were dishonest.

infer: to draw a conclusion

From the evidence, Jack *inferred* that we had been in the cabin.

its/it's

its: the possessive of *it*

He placed the book in *its* proper place.

it's: contraction of *it is* or *it has*

It's been a long day and we all ought to go to bed.

knew/new

knew: past tense of *know*

Bill *knew* where the secret panel was located.

new: recent or additional

Who's the *new* girl in school?

know/no

know: to perceive, understand (verb)

I *know* where they've hidden the presents this year.

no: not so (adverb)

No, I can't do it.

not any, not one (adjective)

Karen took *no* chances.

later/latter

later: after the expected time (adverb)

I'll have to see you *later*.

latter: the second of two things (noun)

Frank took the former, but I chose the *latter*.

closer to the end (adjective)

It was during the *latter* part of the evening that I left.

lay/lie

lay: to put, place (takes an object)

He *lays* his hat on the table.

lie: to recline; be situated

Wanda often *lies* down after dinner.

lead/lead/led

lead: the metal (noun)

The bullets were made of *lead.*

lead: to guide, show the way (verb)

The usher will *lead* you to your seats.

led: past tense of *lead*

He *led* me beside the still waters.

loan/lone

loan: a sum of money lent at interest; something lent (noun)

The bank manager signed my *loan.*

lone: isolated, sole (adjective)

Jane was the *lone* doctor in town.

loose/lose

loose: not fastened or restrained (adjective)

Harry's clothes were old and *loose.*

lose: to fail to find, win, or keep (verb)

She's going to *lose* her position.

mail/male

mail: letter (noun)

to send letters (verb)

He *mailed* the packages and picked up his *mail* at the post office.

male: masculine (noun/ adjective)

How do you know it's a *male* bird?

meat/meet

meat: food (noun)

He doesn't eat *meat* any more.

meet: to come upon, be present at (verb)

We've got to *meet* her bus this afternoon.

miner/minor

miner: person who works in a mine (noun)

Twenty-nine *miners* were lost in the mine accident.

minor: under legal age (noun) lesser, smaller (adjective)

That he's a *minor* is a *minor* matter.

pain/pane

pain: the sensation of hurting

I have a *pain* in my elbow.

pane: piece of glass in a window or door

The baseball broke three *panes* of glass.

pair/pare/pear

pair: two similar items (noun)

Dan bought a *pair* of cockatoos.

pare: to peel, remove the outer
    skin (verb)

Sarah *pared* the apple slowly.

pear: fruit (noun)

I had a *pear* and two oranges
for lunch.

passed/past

passed: past tense of *pass:* to
       move on or ahead (verb)

He *passed* his math test.

past: over, gone by (adjective)

This *past* week was rough.

    the time before the
    present (noun)

History is the study of the *past.*

peace/piece

peace: the absence of war or
    disagreement

Charles is really trying to
make *peace* with us.

piece: a portion or part of
    something

Joan ate three *pieces* of Grandma's pumpkin pie.

peal/peel

peal: a ringing of bells; loud
    noise (noun)

I heard *peals* of laughter coming from the classroom.

    to ring; to make a loud
    noise (verb)

The bells *pealed* when the war
ended.

peel: the skin, rind of an orange
    or banana (noun)

Don't step on that *peel!*

    to strip; pare (verb)

Harold *peeled* off his wet
clothes.

peer/pier

peer: an equal (noun)

Laurence Olivier has no *peer.*

    to look intently (verb)

Why is he *peering* at me so
strangely?

pier: a platform extending from
    the shore over water
    (noun)

Will is down at the *pier* fishing.

personal/personnel

personal: private, one's own
    (adjective)

I'd never say anything *personal*
to Mr. Wilson.

personnel: the people in an organization (noun)

You'll have to talk to Ms.
Jones, our *personnel* manager.

plain/plane

plain: open; clear; simple
    (adjective)

Ann wore a *plain* dress with
pearls.

    an extensive, broad, tree-
    less area (noun)

Animals roamed the *plain.*

plane: an airplane; a flat, level surface; a carpenter's tool (noun)

Betsy took the *plane* to Des Moines this afternoon.

precede/proceed

precede: to come before in time or rank

Mrs. Waters *preceded* me into the room.

proceed: to go forward

The teacher *proceeded* to read us all the rules.

prejudice/prejudiced

prejudice: preconceived idea; bias (noun)

Shane has a *prejudice* against lawyers.

to cause someone to judge prematurely (verb)

His testimony may very well *prejudice* the jury.

prejudiced: past participle of *prejudice* (adjective)

The *prejudiced* man had a hatred of children.

principal/principle

principal: first; highest; chief (adjective)

the head of a school; money, capital (noun)

The *principal* deciding factor was that the high school *principal* did not have to put down any *principal* to purchase the house.

principle: a truth; rule; standard (noun)

One of my *principles* has to do with telling the truth.

quiet/quite

quiet: silent, still (adjective)

The room was very *quiet.*

quite: completely, really (adverb)

Paul's house was *quite* small.

read/read/red

read: to interpret written symbols; to grasp the meaning of (verb)

How many books can you *read* in a month?

read: past tense of *read* (verb)

He *read* the book last week.

red: the color (adjective)

Red is my favorite color.

regardless

regardless: in spite of everything, anyway (adverb)

Do not write as *irregardless.* Write "We're going *regardless.*"

right/rite/write

right: just; correct; desirable (adjective)

Mary had just the *right* outfit on.

the right-hand side or direction (noun)

The car swerved to the *right.*

rite: religious or ceremonial act or custom (noun)

We all went to the last *rites* for Mr. Fletcher.

write: to compose, draw, or communicate (verb)

If you don't *write* me by next week, you're in trouble.

road/rode/rowed

road: path, course (noun)

The *road* to stardom is long and hard.

rode: past tense of ride (verb)

The cowboys *rode* into the sunset.

rowed: past tense of *row* (verb)

Clyde *rowed* across the lake.

role/roll

role: part or function (noun)

My *role* in the play is not large.

roll: to move forward as on wheels (verb)

Gene *rolled* out of the bar after midnight.

something rolled; list of names; bread (noun)

Mrs. Tirrell read the *roll*.

root/route

root: base, origin

We found the *root* of the problem.

route: road, course

What *route* will you take?

sail/sale

sail: to travel by water (verb)

Let's *sail* to Tahiti.

the material used to catch the wind in sailing (noun)

The *sails* of the ship hung limply in the humid air.

sale: the exchange of goods or services for money (noun)

I bought a whole set of dishes at that garage *sale*.

scene/seen

scene: view, setting, display (noun)

It was a frightening *scene*.

seen: past participle of *see*

Wendy's cat has not been *seen* for over three weeks.

sew/so/sow

sew: to make or repair with needle and thread (verb)

You really ought to *sew* that hole in your sweater.

so: thus, likewise, consequently, to such an extent (adverb)

We were tired, so we left.

She was so late that we began to worry.

sow: to scatter seed (verb)

As ye *sow*, so shall ye reap.

sole/soul

sole: part of the foot or shoe; fish (noun)

He had a large nail in the *sole* of his boot.

single, only one (adjective) | The court has the *sole* right to determine this case.

soul: spirit; spiritual part or nature (noun) | The preacher was convinced he was saving *souls.*

stationary/stationery
stationary: not moving (adjective) | The train was *stationary.*

stationery: writing paper, envelopes (noun) | I'm going to the *stationery* store on my way to lunch.

tail/tale
tail: end, rear | The *tail* of the kite whipped around his head.

tale: a report, story | Eric told *tales* of his college days.

than/then
than: in comparison with | I would rather dance *than* sleep.

then: referring to time | I was younger *then.*

their/there/they're
their: the possessive of *they* (pronoun) | I really admire *their* courage.

there: in that place or time (adverb) | I don't want to go *there.*

also used to introduce a clause or sentence (pronoun) | *There* are three suspects.

they're: contraction of *they are* | *They're* coming back here after the game.

thorough/threw/through
thorough: complete, careful (adjective) | They conducted a *thorough* search of the grounds.

threw: past tense of *throw* (verb) | The judge *threw* the book at him.

through: in, among (preposition) | He went *through* the door.

though/thought
though: although, however | I'll go, *though* I don't want to.

thought: past tense of *think* (verb) | I *thought* you said you loved me.

the act or product of thinking (noun) | Bob doesn't have a *thought* in his head.

to/too/two

to: toward (preposition); marks infinitive of a verb	She went *to* the store *to* shop.
too: also; more than; very (adverb)	You really work *too* hard.
two: the number (noun)	Our team had only *two* singles.

used to

used to: indicates a former state, habitual practice, or custom	Never write as *use to*. Write "Dick *used to* smoke two packs a day."

wear/were/we're/where

wear: to have on clothes (verb)	The Westons *wear* expensive clothes.
were: past tense of *be* (verb)	*Were* you home last night?
we're: contraction of *we are*	*We're* leaving now.
where: location (adverb)	*Where* are your mittens?

weather/whether

weather: atmospheric conditions (noun)	What's the *weather* forecast for tomorrow?
whether: used to introduce alternatives (conjunction)	I don't know *whether* I'll go or not.

who's/whose

who's: contraction of *who is* or *who has*	*Who's* going to the dance next week?
whose: the possessive of *who* (adjective)	*Whose* woods these are I think I know.

your/you're

your: possessive form of *you* (adjective)	*Your* driving is awful.
you're: contraction of *you are*	If you don't get in here right now, *you're* going to be sorry.

SPELLING SKILLS

Spelling is a problem for many people; even experienced writers must use a dictionary to check their spelling.

The following techniques can help solve your spelling difficulties:

1. Increase the amount of reading you do; this will help you identify misspelled words in your own writing and will improve your overall spelling skills.

2. In your Writer's Notebook, keep a list of words you frequently misspell.

Spelling List

confident   con fi(dent)

maintenance   main te (nance)

consistent   con sis (tent)

receive   re (ceive)

Writing Assignment   On a separate page of your Writer's Notebook, keep a list of words you misspell. Look up the word in a dictionary and list the *correct* version of the word. Break the word into syllables and circle the part that is giving you trouble. As the list grows, look for patterns. Put a check beside words that are a repeat problem. Identify particular spelling problems such as word endings, doubled consonants, and i/e combinations.

Answer Key for Chapter 9

Exercise 1
page 143   *Combining Sentences Using Coordinating Words*

Notice that in some sentences, more than one coordinating word will work.

1. She left to go to work, and I stayed home to fix dinner. (You could also use *so* or *but.*)
2. The printer may be purchased with the computer, but it may also be added to the system later. (You could also use *and* or *or.*)
3. The pilot whale was firmly beached in the shallow water near the jetty, yet it was still alive. (You could also use *and* or *but.*)
4. I was reluctant to have him work on my car, for he seemed to have a careless attitude.
5. Her father died two months before she was born, so she never knew him. (You could also use *and.*)

Exercise 2
page 143   *Revising Writing by Combining Sentences Using Coordinating Words*

The sentences in this paragraph may be connected in a variety of ways, so your revision of the passage will probably be different from the one below.

> We left the car parked in the shade of a tree. We couldn't lock it because of the jammed window, so we took along the camera. We locked the tape deck in the trunk. The day was overcast, but it was hot, and we began to sweat as soon as we started walking. I asked Susan how far it was to her aunt's cabin, for I had never been there before. Susan said it was only about three quarters of a mile. It was all uphill, or at least it seemed that way.

Exercise 3
page 146   *Combining Sentences with Subordinating Words*

The sentences in this exercise may be joined using different subordinating conjunctions; therefore, your responses will probably differ from the ones below. Remember, you need to provide two revisions if possible.

1. *Revision 1:* Because interest rates fell, stock prices soared.

   Revision 2: When interest rates fell, stock prices soared.

2. *Revision 1:* Because the water in the goldfish bowl was not changed for two months, the goldfish all died.

   Revision 2: The goldfish all died when the water in their bowl was not changed for two months.

3. *Revision 1:* When radar spotted an intruding aircraft, fighters scrambled to intercept it.

   Revision 2: Fighters scrambled to intercept an intruding aircraft after radar spotted it.

4. *Revision 1:* The checks were inserted before the envelopes were taped shut.

   Revision 2: The envelopes were taped shut after the checks were inserted.

5. *Revision 1:* Although the gymnast suffered a shoulder injury, she kept her scholarship.

   Revision 2: The gymnast kept her scholarship until she suffered a shoulder injury.

Exercise 4
page 148   *Combining Sentences Using Relative Pronouns*

1. The bridge, which had been overloaded with truck traffic for years, finally collapsed.
2. Phillip, who needed only fifteen more units to receive his degree, had to quit school to take care of his mother.
3. High-fat diets, which are common in America, have been associated with increased risk of heart disease.
4. Tommy, who had a habit of helping himself to other people's food, was not the most popular boy at the academy.
5. The fire, which had not been tended during the night, was dead by morning.
6. The parents, whose boy was the only one still missing, sat slumped against the far wall of the cabin.
7. The hospital, which is the sole provider of medical services for much of the inner-city population, faces severe reductions under the terms of the new budget.
8. My uncle, who was forced to retire after his sixty-fifth birthday, cannot support himself on his Social Security benefits.
9. The party, which had gotten off to a slow start, continued for the entire Labor Day weekend.

10. My father, who was highly allergic to formaldehyde, broke into a rash whenever he entered the anatomy building.

11. The home computer, which had been purchased to solve problems, soon was causing squabbles over who could use it.

12. The small four-cylinder engine, which had originally been designed to power farm machinery, proved to be a winner when it was installed in the Lotus.

Exercise 5
page 150   *Combining Sentences Using Relative Pronouns*

1. *Revision 1:* I had not seen Bianca, who seemed thinner and grayer and even more beautiful, for some time.

   Revision 2: Bianca, whom I had not seen for some time, seemed thiner and grayer and even more beautiful.

2. *Revision 1:* The studio, which was rather barren, looked out over a wet garden full of bright new daffodils.

   Revision 2: The studio, which looked out over a wet garden full of bright new daffodils, was rather barren.

3. *Revision 1:* The child, who could not have been older than four, stood clutching her father's legs.

   Revision 2: The child, who stood clutching her father's legs, could not have been older than four.

4. *Revision 1:* The cut, which required more than thirty stitches to close, ran down her thumb and across her palm.

   Revision 2: The cut, which ran down her thumb and across her palm, required more than thirty stitches to close.

5. *Revision 1:* The lecturer, who continued to talk at the audience for another forty minutes, was a well-known bore.

   Revision 2: The lecturer, who was a well-known bore, continued to talk at the audience for another forty minutes.

Exercise 6
page 152   *Modifying Sentences with Relative Pronouns*

The sentences in this exercise may be expanded with a variety of modifiers; therefore, your responses will differ from the ones below. Remember, you need two variations of each sentence.

1. Miss Millet, who had been at Barkley School for twenty-five years, was my teacher in first grade.

   Miss Millet, who spit out her words at us in perpetual fury, was my teacher in first grade.

2. The football team, which had drafted an all-star quarterback, was confident.

The football team, whose coach had just delivered a pep talk, was confident.

3. The dinner, which had been scorching on the stove for half an hour, was no longer edible.

The dinner, which the dog had freely sampled while Mother gathered us to the table, was no longer edible.

4. The train, which was carrying naphtha in tank cars, caught fire.

The train that took us from Pueblo to Gallup caught fire.

Exercise 7
page 153   *Adding Phrases*

1. Thick with rust, the key would no longer fit the lock.
2. Soft and overripe, the cheese had a rotten smell.
3. Oozy and red, the baby's eyes were severely infected.
4. Full of round white rocks, the meadow was nearly a quarter-mile wide at this point.
5. Heavy with eggs, the mayfly was trapped in the surface film of the pond.
6. The bus driver, a patient man, is always willing to answer questions about routes and transfers.
7. Sandra, a poor swimmer, never made it to shore.
8. His father, a member of the U.S. cycling team at the 1952 Olympics, still takes long bicycle trips each weekend.
9. Rhonda, a frequent visitor to Mexico, loves to bargain with the shopkeepers.
10. My roommate, a real pack rat, never throws anything away.
11. Lifting up the lid, we peered inside.
12. Sweeping to the left, the fullback made a seven-yard gain.
13. Diving suddenly, the gull snapped up a fish.
14. Still burning out of control, the fire threatened a convalescent hospital.
15. Arguing loudly, the two men disappeared down the street.
16. In the spring we moved back to Cincinnati.
17. The prime minister, under pressure from the U.S. State Department, eventually agreed to lift the trade restrictions.
18. After his birthday, he began going to the quarterhorse races every night.

19. The truck, in poor repair, broke down within twenty miles.

20. All students must pass a comprehensive writing exam before graduating.

Exercise 8
page 156   *Revising with Reduced Sentences*

The paragraph may be revised in a variety of ways.

> The mill, an L-shaped two-story structure, stands on the south side of Jedadiah Creek. Its roof, thatched and steeply pitched, needs repairs where the chestnut tree has thrust an arm through it. The solidly timbered walls look as if they could last for another two centuries. The waterwheel, dappled with green patches of moss, continues to slowly revolve, emptying one bucket after another back into the millstream.

Exercise 9
page 157   *Revising a Passage by Combining Sentences*

The paragraph may be revised in a variety of ways, and your own revision will differ from the example given here.

> Franz Ferdinand, the crown prince of Austria, was assassinated June 28, 1914, while he was visiting the town of Sarajevo. As Franz Ferdinand entered the town riding in an open car at the head of the procession, the first assassination attempt was made with a bomb. Although the bomb was accurately thrown, Franz Ferdinand deflected it with his arm, and the bomb exploded behind the car. The incident was unnerving, yet Franz Ferdinand refused to cancel the visit. Security was lax. Army troops who were available to line the parade route were not used because their uniforms were not impressive enough. As the procession continued up the road, Franz Ferdinand's driver missed a turn and had to back up. A second assassin, who was standing nearby, walked up to the car and fired two shots. Franz Ferdinand, who was hit once in the neck, bled to death within a few minutes. Although his last words were, "It is nothing," his assassination helped to trigger World War I.

Exercise 10
page 160   *Making Words Specific*

The sentences in this exercise may be revised in a variety of ways; therefore, your responses will most likely differ from the ones below. Remember, you need to provide two revisions.

1. *Revision 1:* This bed has bedbugs.
   Revision 2: This apartment has leaky plumbing.

2. *Revision 1:* Lou slurped his milk.

   Revision 2: Manda gulped the carrot juice.

3. *Revision 1:* I am allergic to dust, dog and cat hair, peanut butter, papayas, and shellfish.

   Revision 2: I am allergic to all synthetic fibers and all milk products.

4. *Revision 1:* His truck needs a new radiator.

   Revision 2: His 1958 T-Bird needs a new paint job.

5. *Revision 1:* My refrigerator is filled with luncheon meat and bread.

   Revision 2: My refrigerator is filled with lasagne.

6. *Revision 1:* We regularly watch *M.A.S.H.* reruns.

   Revision 2: We regularly watch *Dallas, Masterpiece Theater,* and *60 Minutes.*

7. *Revision 1:* The police officer lectured the tight-lipped taxi driver.

   Revision 2: The police officer consoled the frantic parent.

Group Activity 1
page 162   *Expanding Sentences*

Responses to this exercise will vary widely. You may want to compare your answers with those of other members of your group or class.

Group Activity 2
page 163   *Expanding Sentences*

Responses to this exercise will vary widely. You may want to compare your answers with those of other members of your group or class.

Exercise 11
page 163   *Expanding Sentences*

Because this exercise is open-ended, the following sentences merely indicate possible revisions; your own responses will differ. Remember that you need to do only five sentences rather than the ten given here.

1. The miner, a victim of black lung disease, coughed answers to the visiting doctor's questions.

2. The attorney general declared in a press conference that he would ask for a court order preventing shipments of radioactive waste from entering the state.

3. Aunt Wilma engulfed Ralph in a hot and perfumy hug.

4. The grain elevator, which was the mainstay of a small town's economy, failed when the railroad cut back service.

5. The jazz quartet—piano, drums, bass, and vibes—opened the first set with an old Billy Holliday number.

6. The longshoremen, who were in sympathy with the Solidarity trade union, refused to load any cargoes bound for Poland.

7. Four generations of Mendozas gathered from three states for a huge picnic and a family portrait.

8. The losing soccer team charged for the safety of the clubhouse, hoping they could get there before their fans got to them.

9. The novice climber, having placed one of her pitons in rotten rock, tumbled about twelve feet when the piton pulled out.

10. The overworked waiter, his jacket stained with wine and sweat, finally returned to our table, bringing cold spaghetti and a warm salad.

Exercise 12
page 165   *Revising a Paragraph*

The paragraph may be revised in a number of ways, and your own revision will certainly differ from the example given here.

> The trip was a disaster. We overslept by two hours, so we had to hurry to get the car loaded, and we forgot to pack the camera and our hiking boots. Even though we skipped breakfast, we didn't get on the road until 7:30, which meant that we got caught in the morning rush-hour traffic. John and Denise, who were in the front seat, got into a long argument over who was responsible for leaving behind the camera, and neither of them noticed when we drove past the turnoff for Lake Tahoe. When we discovered that we had gone too far, we tried to take a short cut over to the road we needed to be on, but we ran out of gas just before we reached it. John grabbed the gas can and stomped off to a filling station, but when he got back we couldn't find the spout to the can, so we spilled about half the fuel and barely had enough to get the car to the station. By this time it was noon, so after we filled up the tank we drove down the street to a truck stop for lunch. We had to wait thirty minutes for the waitress to bring our food, and the hamburgers and fries were cold and tasteless by the time they arrived. As soon as we got back on the road, rain started to splatter against the windshield, but the wiper on the driver's side flopped uselessly from side to side, blurring rather than clearing the windshield. We pulled over to fix it, and by the time I got it repaired my jacket and pants were soaked through. We didn't arrive at the cabins until nearly midnight and we had to wake up the manager to let us in. He was almost as grumpy and ill-tempered as we were.

Exercise 13
page 166   *Getting Rid of Deadwood*

Answers to this exercise will vary.

1. It is my belief that it is of great importance for the college student to set up a schedule that involves studying on a regular basis in order

to get <u>assignments</u> in <u>on time</u> when they are due, and especially <u>long-term projects.</u>

College students should study regularly so that they can submit assignments (and especially long-term projects) on time.

2. <u>My</u> future <u>plans</u> involve a very extended <u>trip</u> over a period of time with a close personal <u>friend</u> of mine.
I plan to take a long trip with a friend.

3. In my opinion, there are a number of reasons why I think <u>we</u> <u>don't</u> really need to consider <u>going</u> during the month of <u>January.</u>
We shouldn't go in January.

4. After careful thought <u>I</u> have come to the final conclusion that at this time we have more than <u>enough</u> natural resources and alternative fuel supplies <u>to overcome</u> the supposedly threatening <u>energy</u> crisis.
I think we have enough energy reserves to overcome the present shortages.

Exercise 14
page 168   *Revising IT IS and THERE ARE Constructions*

Responses to this exercise may vary.

1. Mandy arrived late in the afternoon.
2. Two children were playing basketball in the school yard.
3. A complex chemical process causes trees to shed their leaves.
4. The engine always made a muffled knocking sound until the car was thoroughly warmed up.
5. This room is hot.

Exercise 15
page 169   *Tightening Passive Sentences*

Responses may vary.

1. The captain caused the accident.
2. The night custodian discovered the body.
3. The company does not hire inexperienced workers.
4. The trout took the bait.
5. The new manager immediately changed the organization of the quality control unit.

Answer Key for Chapter 10

Skills Check, page 176

capitalization _____

My First job [J]

consistent
verb tense _____

I folded the newspaper neatly and wrap [wrapped] a rubber

band around it so that it would not fly open when

pronoun
agreement _____

I threw them [it] on the porch. When I had finished)

wrapping all sixty newspapers[;] I loaded them on

incomplete
sentence _____

my little red wagon and started to distribute

run-together
sentences _____

them to my customers. It was not a hard job, it [but]

was not an easy one either.

One of the hard parts was delivering in the

wintertime when the temperature dropped below

incomplete
sentence _____

freezing and the snow was two to three feet deep,

Too [t] deep to walk in. I wear [wore] thick clothing,

consistent
verb tense _____

usually more than two layers. Even though I could

irregular
verb form _____

keep my body warm, my face would froze [freeze]. After

being outside for a while, my face would become

comma usage _____

numb from the chilly air. Pulling the wagon

through the thick snow was tough. Most of the

comma usage _____

time I would have to leave my wagon at a corner,

non-parallel
sentence _____

pick up several newspapers, distribute them, and

then pulling [pull] the wagon through the next block.

247

The cold was not the only difficulty. I had to

be on the alert constantly for dogs. Usually

run-together sentence _____ people did not let their dogs out in the wintertime, *but* ∧

in the summertime various sizes of dogs

consistent verb tense _____ *roamed* ~~roam~~ the streets, posing great problems for

paper boys and mailmen.

capitalization _____ Another problem that *I* had to deal with was

collecting money at the end of the week. Most

incomplete sentence _____ people paid on time, but there *were* some who would

pronoun agreement _____ delay ~~his~~ *their* payments for as long as four weeks. It

was really annoying finding them not at home *or*

incomplete sentence _____ hearing them say that they would have the money

in a week or two. Usually I would not wrap rubber

bands around their newspapers—not until they

had paid the bill.

comma and semicolon usage _____ Despite all of these problems*;*

delivering newspapers was a good experience. I

learned a lot about people and how to deal with

run-together sentence _____ them*;* I also learned to handle money properly and

to take responsibilities. It was a good start for

me in learning about life.

Exercise 1
page 178   *Identifying Complete Sentences by Using the Complete Idea Test*

1. | A policeman drove us around the huge parking lot looking for the car. |

Complete.

2. And to the Fourth of July picnic in Crescent City, which was best of all.

   Not complete. The word group does not indicate who went to the picnic, nor what took place there.

3. Although I called several times and even left a note in the screen door.

   Not complete. "Although" the person called, what happened? We cannot tell; the word group is an incomplete sentence.

4. My cat hates windy days.

   Complete.

5. She staring at the floor for a long time.

   Not complete. This doesn't explain what "she" did. Notice that it would be easy to make this a complete sentence: "She *was* staring at the floor for a long time," or "She *has* been staring at the floor for a long time."

6. Dropped it on the deck.

   Not complete. This word group does not indicate *who* "dropped it on the deck."

7. Which was why we didn't get along.

   Not complete. What does the "which" refer to? Notice that the sentence would be complete if "this" was used instead of "which": "*This* was why we didn't get along."

8. Asking if I was sure that I'd done the job right.

   Not complete. This does not indicate who was "asking."

9. The whole afternoon was wasted.

   Complete.

10. Because I had already proven myself working as an intern in the blueprint department during the summer.

    Not complete. The word group leaves us hanging: What happens "because I had already proven myself . . ."?

Exercise 2
page 180   *Identifying Complete Sentences by Using the Subject-Verb Test*

1. Not complete. This word group contains neither a subject nor a verb part.

2. Not complete. The verb part is incomplete or missing: The foxes sitting beside the log.

3. Complete. Soft drinks rot teeth.

4. Not complete. The verb part is missing: <u>Maude, who dislikes children.</u>

5. Not complete. The subject is missing: <u>Sat down and cried.</u>

6. Complete. <u>Poetry is a mystery to me.</u>

7. Not complete. This word group contains neither a subject nor a verb part.

8. Complete. <u>I attended every class.</u>

9. Not complete. The verb part is missing: <u>The theory that the sun, not the earth, is the center of the solar system.</u>

10. Not complete. The word group contains neither a subject nor a verb part.

Exercise 3
page 181   *Constructing Complete Sentences*

One set of correct complete sentences is given below; your set of sentences may vary from this without being incorrect.

1. Correct braking techniques help prevent skidding, even in panic stops.

2. As the curtain rose on the darkened stage, a hush swept across the audience.

3. The poverty and deprivation of his childhood, things he never talked openly about, influenced the kind of adult he became.

4. Swimming is a sport in which an amateur is unlikely to suffer injuries.

5. Graciously extending her hand, the mayor walked toward her defeated opponent.

6. Long ago though it was, the scandal caused by the Chicago White Sox in the 1919 World Series is still controversial.

7. He straightened his tie, took a deep breath, and walked briskly into the courtroom.

8. Films such as *Hearts and Minds* (1974), *The Deer Hunter* (1978), *Coming Home* (1978), and *Platoon* (1986) helped shape the American public's image of the Vietnam War.

9. The reaction of most parents to groups such as the Beastie Boys is easy to predict.

10. Peanuts, almonds, raisins, and sunflower seeds are nutritious snacks.

Exercise 4
page 183   *Identifying and Correcting Incomplete Sentences*

The paragraph may be correctly revised in a variety of ways. One correct revision is given below; your own revision may differ from it without being incorrect.

> She sat before the window, rigid and still, like a cat waiting for a mouse. The clock ticked in the darkened hallway and finally startled her when it chimed out the hour. It was two o'clock. She turned on the light, shook her head, and shuffled off to the kitchen, where she opened the refrigerator door. A note was inside.

Exercise 5
page 185   *Correcting Run-Together Sentences*

1. The soap operas were an escape from the emptiness of her life. My aunt watched them every day.

   The soap operas were an escape from the emptiness of her life; my aunt watched them every day.

   The soap operas were an escape from the emptiness of her life, and my aunt watched them every day. ("so" could be used in place of "and")

   Because the soap operas were an escape from the emptiness of her life, my aunt watched them every day.

2. Children growing up in career military families move frequently. Studies show military children are as well adjusted as other children.

   Children growing up in career military families move frequently; studies show military children are as well adjusted as other children.

   Children growing up in career military families move frequently, but studies show military children are as well adjusted as other children.

   Although children growing up in career military families move frequently, studies show military children are as well adjusted as other children.

Exercise 6
page 186   *Correcting Run-Together Sentences*

The paragraph may be correctly revised in a variety of ways. One correct revision is given below; your own revision may differ from it without being incorrect.

When I came to, I couldn't feel anything in my right leg; the left leg hurt terribly, however. I could see that the bone was broken. It was pushing up the skin, and a huge bruise was forming. My arms were OK, and I could sit up. I remember being thankful that I had not broken my back. I gingerly patted my head to see if everything was still in one piece. It was sore and my lips were bloody, but I couldn't find any serious damage.

Exercise 7
page 187   *Correcting Nonparallel Sentences*

Your answers may vary, depending upon the form of parallelism you choose to use.

1. Losing the car keys made me feel angry, stupid, and fearful.
2. We spent the summer playing, partying, and going to the beach.
3. Fame, power, and money were Teresa's only goals.
4. She liked reading novels much more than studying for tests or preparing her lab assignments.
5. Our quarterback had a sprained thumb, a pulled hamstring, and a broken toe.

Exercise 8
page 189   *Revising for Consistent Tense*

This revision is based on the present tense, since the paragraph discusses things that wombats *usually* do.

The wombat, one of several pouched mammals, lives in Australia and Tasmania. It resembles a small bear and reaches the size of a large dog. Like the kangaroo, the wombat first lives in its mother's pouch. Later, it inhabits tunnels. The wombat feeds on grass, roots, and bark. Strangely, the wombat's woodchuck-like teeth are not worn down with chewing and gnawing; they continue to grow throughout the wombat's life.

Exercise 9
page 191   *Identifying Tenses*

infinitive

In order to lose weight, I have decided to walk more. When I was in college,

past

I walked everywhere I went, and consequently I never had a problem with

present

my weight. Now I walk only when I must. My new resolution is that I will

future   *present perfect*

walk at least two miles a day. My plan is going well: I have walked over ten

future perfect

miles so far this week, and if I keep on schedule I will have walked *past perfect*

fourteen miles by Sunday. It was a good feeling to know that I had walked

two miles this morning before my regular jelly doughnut.

Exercise 10
page 191
Using Verb Tenses

The correct verb form for each tense is given below. The actual sentences will vary.

1. Present	start	
2. Past	started	
3. Future	will start	
4. Present perfect	have started	
5. Past perfect	had started	
6. Future perfect	will have started	

Exercise 11
page 194
Subject-Verb Agreement

1. Flame <u>glows</u> blue at its center and <u>burns</u> orange at the fringe.
2. In the valley, smoke <u>curls</u> from the chimney of a lone cabin.
3. The spring and summer <u>pass</u> quickly.
4. A goldfish two inches long <u>requires</u> at least two gallons of water.
5. The police commander in each of the twenty substations <u>reports</u> directly to the chief.
6. That picture of the boys <u>captures</u> their expressions perfectly.
7. The branches of the tall old oak tree <u>wave</u> in the wind.
8. The students' pencils <u>scratch</u> across the page and never <u>rest</u> even for a minute.
9. According to the family agreement, Paul and Jean <u>scrub</u> the kitchen and bathroom floors, and Brenda <u>dusts</u> all the furniture each week.
10. She and I always <u>enjoy</u> going to summer concerts.
11. A human skeleton <u>contains</u> 206 bones.
12. Whales <u>filter</u> tiny plants and animals from sea water with a mouth fringed <u>with</u> strainers called baleen.
13. The color of the acids <u>changes</u> quickly.
14. The stunt plane <u>spins</u> in the air and <u>dives</u> toward the crowd.
15. Our cat always <u>jumps</u> at spots on the wall.
16. Susan or Kay <u>plans</u> to be at the meeting.

17. Living on the streets of this city <u>are</u> hundreds of young teenagers.

18. There <u>are</u> several safety rules that must be followed in this factory.

19. Either your driver's license or a major credit card <u>is</u> acceptable identification for cashing a check.

Exercise 12
page 199   *Using the Present, Past, and Past Participle of Irregular Verbs*

1. I <u>am</u> ready to leave now. I <u>was</u> ready several hours ago. In fact, I have <u>been</u> ready all week.

2. The dogs <u>bite</u> anyone who tries to come in the yard. Rover <u>bit</u> the mail carrier last week, and now we have to pick up our mail at the post office. The statistics on the number of postal workers who have been <u>bitten</u> in the past year are alarming.

3. On Sundays I <u>lie</u> on the sofa all morning. Last week was worse than usual: I <u>lay</u> around all day. The problem with this laziness is that after I have <u>lain</u> around like this, I have no energy.

4. My children constantly <u>lose</u> their jackets. Last week Sammy <u>lost</u> a jacket and a sweater. They have <u>lost</u> so many jackets that I'm having trouble finding money to buy new ones.

5. The bell <u>rings</u> every morning and summons the reluctant students. Yesterday when it <u>rang,</u> one group in the far corner of the playground paid no attention. Not until the final tardy bell had <u>rung</u> did those students slowly start toward their classes.

6. Please <u>lay</u> the money above the cash register drawer as you make change. Yesterday when you <u>laid</u> the money in the drawer, a customer accused you of short-changing her. If you had <u>laid</u> the money above the drawer, you would not have had a problem.

Exercise 13
page 200   *Irregular Verb Forms*

1. They <u>hanged</u> the rustler.
2. He had <u>hung</u> the painting.
3. The horse had <u>lain</u> down in the meadow.
4. The chicken had <u>laid</u> four eggs.
5. The sail <u>lay</u> upon the deck.
6. The pants had <u>shrunk</u> four inches.
7. Tom and Huck had <u>sworn</u> an oath.
8. The guide <u>led</u> them to the hut.

9. They had <u>risen</u> early.

10. Carol had <u>lent</u> him the money.

11. They had <u>hidden</u> (or <u>hid</u>) the money.

12. She <u>dealt</u> the cards.

13. Mother had <u>fallen</u> asleep.

14. Marsha <u>grew</u> three inches that summer.

15. The ice <u>burst</u> the pipes.

Exercise 14
page 201   *Identifying Pronouns*

1. The berries of the festive Christmas plant mistletoe are deceiving; they are highly poisonous.

2. Venus is not difficult to identify; it is almost always the brightest star in the sky.

3. For protection, the mail carrier totes a mace cartridge in a holster hooked to his belt. He reports he has never had to use the weapon because nothing has ever attacked him.

4. The Tassles took their dog, Julie, to pet obedience school, but she was immediately suspended for her bad behavior.

5. The actor complained, "I could have been a star, but the director didn't like me and cut my part."

Exercise 15
page 202   *Correcting Pronoun Agreement Problems*

1. The wall map in my den indicates which European countries share their boundaries with Communist countries.

2. John continued to talk even though I told him that he should stop.

3. A person who wants to be treated as an adult must take responsibility for his or her actions.

4. The avocado trees in the yard next door are beginning to drop their avocados on our side of the fence.

5. As students get used to college and learn to budget time, they find themselves getting better grades and more sleep.

Exercise 16
page 204   *Correcting Pronoun Shifts*

When I think back to my childhood, I realize that my parents kept my brother and me in line with the help of several mythological characters. For instance, Santa wasn't always the jolly, rotund figure of good cheer that children expect. My parents let us know that our bad behavior might displease Santa. We could get coal in our stockings. Worse yet, we might get only the "little things" on our lists. The boogey man also kept us in line. He helped my parents get us home before dark, for we could be snatched off the sidewalk if we wandered home after the sun had set. Even the Tooth Fairy had her nasty side. She refused to take a tooth with a cavity in it. We brushed regularly, knowing that if we didn't, a rotten tooth would still be under the pillow in the morning.

Exercise 17
page 207   *Using a Comma Before a Joining Word*

1. Children's toys are now the product of painstaking research, and development costs for one toy can run into the millions of dollars.
2. The cheetah can run an amazing seventy miles per hour, but it can maintain this speed only for short distances.
3. The baby may be coming down with another respiratory infection, or he may have an allergy that has not been identified.

Exercise 18
page 208   *Using a Comma to Set Off an Introductory Word or Word Group*

1. After the boss carefully explained the new procedures, we were less confused.
2. In the winter of 1982–83, heavy rains caused the river to flood.
3. Yes, I agree with your decision.

Exercise 19
page 210   *Using Commas to Set Off Words or Word Groups That Interrupt the Flow of a Sentence*

1. The facts, therefore, do not support your conclusions.
2. My brother-in-law, who is a health fanatic, gets more colds than anyone I know.
3. "The Super Bowl," the sociologist commented, "has become an annual national ritual for millions of Americans."
4. Jim Dorman, the new shop steward, will file a grievance.
5. We pulled into our driveway, happy to be home.

Exercise 20
page 211   *Using Commas to Separate Items in a Series*

1. The sting of a bee, hornet, or wasp can cause a severe reaction in some people.

2. The high desert is a harsh, arid environment.

3. Small cuts should be washed for several minutes with fresh water, covered with a bandage, and watched for signs of infection.

4. Soon the empty parking lot will be jammed, every seat in the stadium will be filled, and the first game of the World Series will begin.

Exercise 21
page 213   *Using Semicolons*

1. Throughout the world, the amount of land covered with forests is decreasing; lumber production, paper making, and firewood gathering are some of the causes of this deforestation.

2. An insufficient supply of vitamin A can cause respiratory, skin, or eye problems; however, an excessive supply of the vitamin also causes problems.

3. I received a high score on the written exam and the oral interview; I believe, therefore, that I have a good chance of getting a job with the fire department.

4. The student who failed the psychology course turned in only two of the four required assignments; furthermore, she did not show up for the final examination.

Exercise 22
page 215   *Using Colons*

1. A number of steps could be taken to reduce fatalities from all-terrain vehicles: require that all ATV operators pass a safety course, make wearing of helmets by operators and passengers mandatory, and regulate where the vehicles may be driven.

2. The following students need to schedule a conference: John Phillips, Christine Brown, and Lewis Garcia.

3. In his 1934 message to Congress, President Roosevelt made the following statement about the arms race: "This grave menace to the peace of the world is due in no small measure to the uncontrolled activities of the manufacturers and merchants of engines of destruction, and it must be met by the concerted action of the peoples of all nations."

Exercise 23
page 217   *Using Dashes and Parentheses*

1. There is one thing you must remember to pack for the camping trip—your sleeping bag.

2. That book on computer programming (which I haven't had time to look at yet) is supposed to be the most helpful guide available. (You would use dashes in this sentence if you wanted to *emphasize* the fact that you had not read the book.)

3. John F. Kennedy (1917–1963) was the youngest person ever elected president of the United States.

4. The diner—with its red Naugahyde booths, Formica-topped tables, and long counter—looked like something right out of the fifties.

Exercise 24
page 218   *Using Hyphens*

My twenty-two-year-old husband, twenty-seven-year-old brother-in-law, and I decided to join a self-help group. Being in the group was a mind-boggling experience. We met for a two-hour session twice a week. Two thirds of the members were very negative; in fact they seemed almost anti-American. One blue-eyed lady with a know-it-all look was especially critical of everything. This self-help group was a disaster: now my husband is my ex-husband.

Exercise 25
page 220   *Using Quotation Marks and Italics or Underlining*

Note: Titles of long works or separate publications are set in *italic* type in published material. When you handwrite or type, you underline these titles.

In my communications class, I was assigned a speech on the topic of leisure activity. I asked my dad for advice. He told me that I should start with a quote from someone famous. I looked at him and said, "Thanks, but where do I look for such a quote?"

He replied, "Try the book *Bartlett's Familiar Quotations,*"

In that book, I found the perfect quote, a line from Mark Twain's *The Adventures of Tom Sawyer:* "Work consists of whatever a body is obliged to do, and play consists of whatever a body is not obliged to do." Next I read an article called "New Uses for Leisure Time" in our local newspaper, *The Daily Chronicle.* I found another article entitled "The Psychological Benefits of Exercise" in the magazine *Psychology Today.* With the information from these articles and my own ideas, I had enough material for my speech.

Exercise 26
page 223   *Using Apostrophes*

1. There's a campaign meeting tonight, but I'm not sure whose turn it is to supply refreshments.

2. That man looks after his dog better than he does his children. The children's faces are dirty, and one little boy's jacket isn't warm

enough for this weather. The faces of the two little <u>girls</u> have a pinched, thin look. <u>It's</u> not a good situation.

3. <u>Isn't</u> that <u>Joe's</u> truck parked next to the <u>neighbor's</u> house?

4. The <u>waitress'</u> uniform <u>wasn't</u> very clean. The food <u>didn't</u> come for over an hour. That restaurant certainly has <u>its</u> problems.

5. <u>John's</u> career plans are still vague.

Acknowledgments

Page 16: From "Physical Violence Aside, TV's Psychic Violence Is the Real Cause for Alarm" by Herbert Kohl. This first appeared in *The Los Angeles Times* on May 21, 1982. Reprinted by permission.

Page 18: Merrill Sheils, "And Man Created the Chip," *Newsweek*, June 30, 1980. Copyright 1980, Newsweek, Inc. All rights reserved. Reprinted by permission.

Page 73: Patrick Huyghe, "Man Bites Man," *OMNI Magazine*, October 1981. Copyright 1981 by OMNI Publications International Ltd., and reprinted with the permission of the copyright owner.

Page 83: From "Desert Solitaire" by Edward Abbey. Reprinted by permission of Don Congdon Associates, Inc. Copyright © 1968 by Edward Abbey.

Dictionary extracts on pp. 85 and 194: © 1982 by Houghton Mifflin Company. Reprinted by permission from *The American Heritage Dictionary of the English Language,* Second College Edition.

Page 93: From "Neutron Weapons: An Agonizing Death" by J. Garrott Allen. This first appeared in *The Los Angeles Times* on November 11, 1981. Reprinted by permission.

Page 95: From "Earth's Ozone Layer Under Freon Siege" by Isaac Asimov, © 1986, The Los Angeles Times Syndicate. Reprinted by permission.

Page 131: Bill Finger, from *North Carolina Independent,* May 23–June 5, 1987 issue. Reprinted by permission.

Index

To the student:

Although it is a published book, *A Guide to the Whole Writing Process* continues to be a work in progress. Please share your experiences with it by completing the questions below. Tear out this page and mail it to:

> Blum/Brinkman/Hoffman/Peck
> c/o Marketing Services
> College Division
> Houghton Mifflin Company
> One Beacon Street
> Boston, Massachusetts 02108

Be honest and specific in your comments. Tell us both what is good and what is bad about *A Guide*. Thank you.

1. Overall, how would you rate *A Guide*? (Check one)
   ( ) excellent   ( ) average
   ( ) good   ( ) poor

2. Which chapters did you find especially helpful? Why? _____

   _____

   _____

   _____

   _____

   _____

3. Which chapters did you find least helpful? Why? _____

   _____

   _____

   _____

   _____

   _____

4. Were any chapters too difficult or confusing? Which ones?

   _____

   _____

5. Do any chapters need more explanation or practices? Which ones and why? _____

   _____

   _____

6. What material would you like to see added to future editions of *A Guide*? _____

    _____

    _____

7. Do you have any additional suggestions, criticisms, or reactions to *A Guide*? _____

    _____

    _____

    _____

    _____

NOTES

NOTES

NOTES

NOTES